RAISING BOYS:
A CHRISTIAN PARENTING BOOK

RAISING BOYS

A CHRISTIAN PARENTING BOOK

A Practical Guide to
Faith-Based Parenting

QUINN KELLY, MS, LMFT

ROCKRIDGE
PRESS

Interior Designer: Alan Carr
Cover Designer: Irene Vandervoort
Art Producer: Megan Baggott
Editor: Carolyn Abate
Production Editor: Ruth Sakata Corley
Production Manager: David Zapanta

Author photo courtesy of Holly Bollinger/Capella Creative

Paperback ISBN: 978-1-63807-208-9
eBook ISBN: 978-1-63807-590-5
R0

This book is dedicated to my four sons, whom I prayed for from the time I was little. You are living proof that God's gifts are the best.

CONTENTS

PART THREE: TARGETED PARENTING STRATEGIES

INTRODUCTION

Hi. My name is Quinn, and I have a huge heart for encouraging parents through any and all parenting circumstances because parenting my four sons (alongside my husband) is the best job I've ever had—but it's also the hardest.

I don't know if you're reading this as a parent at the end of your rope. Or perhaps you're a parent who thinks raising boys is much harder than you imagined. Or maybe you're a parent who wants to improve your parenting game. But whatever life scenario brings you here, I want to sincerely congratulate you for opening this book. Because if you are reading these words, then I already know two impressive things about you. The first is that you are someone who believes parenting your son is important, and the second is that you desire to parent your son in a Christlike way with intention and care. To me, this combination of traits in a parent will help provide a boy with Christian values and habits so he leaves the nest as a Godly and well-adjusted young man.

As you read these words, you may think back to your young son picking his nose at the breakfast table this morning, or you may remember when your adolescent son rolled his eyes and talked back to you before he left for school and wonder, "Is it really possible to raise Godly young men who stand out in this world with integrity? And am I really the parent to do it?"

As a licensed marriage and family therapist and mother, I have asked myself similar questions multiple times over the past 13 years, during particularly hard parenting moments. But every time I get to this place, the Lord reminds me of this same simple truth from Proverbs 3:5–6: "Trust in the Lord with all your heart and lean not on your own understanding; in all your ways submit to him, and he will make your paths straight."

With God by your side, and with your Bible and hopefully this book in hand, you are more than equipped to be the wise and Christ-honoring parent you desire for your son. All you need is a willing heart that is ready to grow with your son and live out the same values you desire to see in him.

As we know, the world we live in can feel daunting. Trying to determine how to shield our sons from influences that will steer them away from our Christian beliefs and values is challenging. Yet as parents, we have an important and hope-filled truth to rest in when we feel unsure about how to protect our sons. It's important to know you will forever be your son's first and most powerful influence. The way you live and the values you teach him serve as buffers of strength and love as he grows.

This book is written to help you build that safeguard of strong Biblical character. In the pages ahead, I will offer practical and Biblical advice to help you discover what traits are at the root of Godly parenting and what parenting principles follow as a result. I'll then end the book with some of my favorite parenting techniques for sons of all ages. Feel free to read this book as a whole, or skip to the parts most relevant to your parenting needs.

Whatever way you read it, just know that I am passionately praying God uses its words to offer you the wisdom you desire so that you can raise the boys God desires in this world.

Cheers to Raising Faith-filled Sons,
Quinn

PART ONE

Raising Boys 101

If you want to know the secret to raising Godly boys, your Bible is the best place to start. In the following sections you'll read about key Biblical parenting principles and a boy's development into manhood. I'll also challenge you to create targeted parenting goals for your own son(s). It's going to be fun, so let's pray and dive in.

1

The Fundamentals of Christian Parenting

I f only the Ten Commandments had a clause that read, "Thou shalt not talk about poop at the table," life would be much easier. Instead, God gives us discernment as we apply His word to our parenting. In this chapter, I will outline some Biblical parenting principles and discuss some of the challenges Christian parents face today.

Parenting Principles from the Bible

Let's face it. There is no perfect parent on this earth. And there never will be. But we can learn a lot about what a perfect parent looks like when we look to God and the way He parents us— His children.

If you aren't familiar with the Israelites in the Bible, they are God's "chosen people" (albeit rebellious) and the ones He desires to become fruitful and multiply. Once Jesus came to earth, the generations that followed and accepted Him into their hearts became grafted into that same "chosen" people. In other words, as Christians we are all God's children. Lucky for us, God is familiar with the challenges that come with parenting.

In Exodus 34:6, God comes down to earth to tell Moses exactly who He is after the Israelites had made the mistake of worshiping a golden calf. He says, "The Lord ... compassionate and gracious God, slow to anger, abounding in love and faithfulness."

This passage is moving because it is clear God wants them to know His heart and His character as their father even after they rebelled. Likewise, we want our children to see those same characteristics in us. So let's dive into some Biblical character traits that make for strong parents.

Love

If you take no other lesson from this book, please make sure you hear this next line with all your heart. The foundation of Godly parenting is love. The Bible teaches us in 1 John 4:8 that "God is love," and if we want our children to know God, then we must lead with love in our parenting.

Because of God's immense love for his children, He sent his only son, Jesus, to die for our sins so we had a way to be set free, forgiven, and close to God. Simply stated, love is where it began for God, and love is where it should begin for us.

When I am able to genuinely show "I love you" to my sons in ways that reach their hearts, they often say "I love you back," not only with their words, but also in the form of respect and willing attentiveness to my expectations for them.

Kindness

If we want to be like God, kindness is key in our parenting. One of my favorite Bible verses is Psalm 127:3, which says, "Children are a heritage from the Lord; offspring a reward from him." I love this verse because it reminds us that children are a gift from God. And I don't know about you, but when I receive a gift, I like to treat it with care. Likewise, we treat our children with care by showing kindness in our words and actions.

Even in times when correction and discipline are necessary, we must be careful not to be needlessly harsh. A child says, "Where are my shoes?" and a parent responds with, "Ugh! You are always losing your shoes!" I encourage you to respond in a way that doesn't make your child feel shame about their mistakes. If God is kind to us when we mess up, then we should seek to mimic that same kindness toward our children.

Patience

We live in a fast-paced world, but Godly parenting is slow and steady. Teaching and building character in children requires immense patience, since much of parenting is often working on the same habits over and over. One of the habits I teach my boys is to pause what they are doing when an adult is trying to engage them in conversation in order to show respect and attentiveness. Yet, building this skill has taken more work than expected because my sons are often ready to quickly move from one activity to the next.

I'll never forget the first day my neighbor walked up to my son and me as we were planting flowers outside. She began asking him questions, and instead of being quiet or disinterested, he engaged with her the whole time. As she walked away, she complimented his manners, and he beamed with pride. I couldn't help but smile, too. It was like God was saying, *"Slow and steady, Quinn."*

Grace and Mercy

To me, these two words go hand in hand and are both so revealing as to who God is to us. By Biblical definition, grace is what we are given—a clean slate through the death of Jesus without deserving it. Mercy is when we are spared the punishment we deserve because of God's love.

As Christian parents we embrace what it means to have God's grace in our lives and in our parenting, so it's only natural that we should extend that same grace to our children when they make a mistake. Lamentations 3:22–23 (ESV) says, "The steadfast love of the Lord never ceases; his mercies never come to an end; they are new every morning; great is your faithfulness."

If God is able to give us a fresh start each morning, then we should also be able to give our children a fresh start with grace and mercy each day, too.

Accountability

The Bible is a book that tells of God's deep love for His children and forgiveness for their shortcomings. Yet in Romans, we also see that God also holds us accountable for our decisions. As a parent, it can be easier to lean into the former statement than the later. It's tempting to think that showing our children grace and mercy means we are supposed to just let them off the hook. However, not holding our children accountable can be harmful to them, as we see in Proverbs 10:17: "Whoever heeds discipline shows the way to life, but whoever ignores correction leads others astray."

Showing our children grace and holding them accountable are not mutually exclusive. Christian parents must hold their children accountable for their decisions and hold themselves accountable, too. I once forgave my son for writing his autograph on my wall in marker—ironically, in his neatest writing ever—but I also chose to never buy him markers again. The next section will dive into this concept a bit more.

Forgiveness

If you are looking for a parenting trait in God that is undeniably woven throughout Scripture, you will find forgiveness. A Godly parent must live with forgiveness on the tip of their tongue and at the forefront of their hearts, because that is exactly what God does for us.

When our fourth son was born, we deemed him our easiest and most angelic baby. However, I'll never forget the day we saw our perfect little angel reach out and hit his brother for the first time. My husband leaned over to me and said, "I guess he just lost angel status." We laughed. We know that part of parenting is understanding that we are raising flawed little humans prone to messing up. And it's our job to teach them through those mistakes and forgive them as we go.

Compassion

Children need compassion. So, the old phrase "kids are resilient" is one I lovingly ask you to put in your mental trash can because it breeds an insensitivity to our children's struggles. Yes, kids are absolutely amazing and can often deal with incredibly tough circumstances, but that doesn't mean it's always easy to be a child.

In stressful moments, it's easy for parents to look at their children and think, "Why are they upset? They've got it made!" We can easily forget that kids are growing and learning daily and their brains are not fully developed like ours. We often assume they know the right way to act, or that they have the emotional maturity to handle their big feelings, but often that's just not true. As Psalm 103:1 tells us, the Lord is compassionate toward us, and we are reminded that we need to be the same for our children.

Joy

Sometimes parenting can feel more like a job than a joy. Even so, it's important to know that God desires you to have joy in both life *and* parenting. God's joy is an incredible strength in parenting, and Psalm 16:11 (ESV) tells us that if we need joy, we can start with Him: "You make known to me the path of life; in your presence there is fullness of joy."

When my first son turned two, I found myself losing joy as a parent because his tantrums were incredibly dramatic. So I prayed about it and asked God to give me joy within my exhaustion. The next time my son lost it over the wrong color sippy cup, instead of frustration, I felt an overwhelming sense of love for this irrational little being with such big feelings. God had given me joy in that moment. And He desires the same for you.

Gentleness

When I was in high school, my mom once asked me if I thought one of my older friends had a good influence on me. She said she'd seen some things in me that she hadn't before I met this group of people, and she wanted to make sure I was remaining true to myself. After that conversation, she didn't do anything more or force me to end the friendship. Instead, she just let me evaluate it on my own. A few months later, I ended the friendship because I could see it wasn't good. I often think back and reflect on how her gentle correction gave me space to grow.

This story reminds me of Ephesians 6:4: "Fathers, do not exasperate your children; instead, bring them up in the training and instruction of the Lord." We often think that kids can exasperate us, but parents can exasperate their kids, too, by being overly critical, angry, and focusing on their flaws instead of their strengths. God encourages us to lead with gentleness.

Faithfulness

The Bible repeatedly displays God's faithfulness to us, and our kids need us to be faithful to them. When I was in high school, I was a cheerleader and tennis player. My dad made sure to never miss a meet or game. So rain or shine, he was always there rooting me on, cheering for me, and always believing I was much more gifted than I actually was. (And he'll still tell you stories of my best tennis match today.)

When I think of my dad, I think of a faithful father who was always there. In the same way, our kids need us to be faithful to them. They need to know that even when we are tired or stressed, our love for them doesn't run out. And if they need us, we show up—ready to bring out the best in them. Because that's what God does for us.

A NUANCED PERSPECTIVE ON AUTHORITY, OBEDIENCE, AND DISCIPLINE

As a licensed marriage and family therapist, I have found there are two primary reasons people feel compelled to listen to an authority figure. One is because they are scared of the authority figure, and knowingly have little power to go against that person. The second is because they respect the authority figure and desire to show it.

As Christians, we know our ultimate authority is God and our children's earthly authority is us—their parent. Sure, the book of Proverbs tells us that the fear of the Lord is the beginning of wisdom. But Godly parents are not focused on using their authority as a way to exert power and control for the sake of it. We know that isn't how God deals with us.

Instead, Godly parents know their job is to use their authority to instill, teach, and protect their children against behaviors and decisions that hurt themselves or others. As parents, we want our children to obey and listen to us out of respect, not fear. If you want your children to be scared of you, then I encourage you to dive into that desire and ask God to reset your heart.

In saying that, teaching children to obey does involve discipline. God forgives His children, but He also holds them accountable. In fact, love without discipline is a far stretch from the love God shows us. As Proverbs 3:11–12 says, "My son, do not despise the Lord's discipline, and do not resent his rebuke, because the Lord disciplines those he loves, as a father the son he delights in." We will discuss more specific methods of discipline in Chapter 8 (page 77).

What It Means to Be a Christian Parent Today

Being a Christian in the 21st century can feel challenging at times. It may seem as if our values are totally different from the messages our children receive from the world around them. It can often feel like we are teaching them one thing and the world is saying the exact opposite. For example:

The world may say, "You do you." But the Bible says, "Honor God."

The world may say, "Make sure to focus on your outside appearance." But God says, "Focus on your heart."

The world may say, "Nothing is bad for you if it makes you happy." But God says, "Sin hurts you and separates you from Me."

It can be easy to tell your child to stand by their faith until you notice their Christian values are causing them to feel alone. But I'm here to encourage and remind you that the Bible's values are not outdated, no matter what. God created each and every one of us, and He still knows what is good for our hearts and minds today—just as much as he did when He created the earth. Similarly, God's ways lead our children to joy and peace, but the world's way—albeit, temporarily enticing—can deplete their minds and spirits.

Our call as Christian parents is to boldly equip our children with confidence to shine bright in a dark world, just like Matthew 5:14 teaches us: "You are the light of the world. A town built on a hill cannot be hidden." And here are some ways we do that.

Christian Parents Know Parenting Is a Growing Process

One of the most beloved parenting verses of all time is from Proverbs 22:6 (ESV): "Train up a child in the way he should go; even when he is old, he will not depart from it." I love this verse. It tells us that Christian parenting is a marathon, not a sprint, because when we train for something, we do it daily and over time. In that same way, children do not build Godly character overnight. Instead, they build it slowly as they receive reinforcement day after day. A wise person once said, "Practice makes progress." The same is true for building faith and character in our children.

Christian Parents Live Out Their Own Faith

If we want our children to grow in their faith, we must grow in our faith, too. We must teach our children about God, not just by telling them about Him, but also by showing them the impact He is making in our own lives. People often ask me why I didn't rebel as a pastor's kid, and I always say, "Because my parents didn't force Jesus on me. Instead, they showed me how much they loved Him." And because of that, I couldn't help but want to know Him, too.

Christian Parents Are Intentional

Therapeutically speaking, intention is one of the primary ways to make relationships healthier and happier. Engaged parents don't just wing it. Instead, they parent with intention, especially when they see things aren't going well. I call these intentional times "parenting resets," a time to evaluate what isn't going well and plan to improve it. Intention can prevent bad habits from taking root.

For example, if I see a spirit of selfishness developing in my home, instead of saying, "Stop being so selfish," I might have my sons help clean each other's rooms. This gives them an opportunity to practice selflessness and experience its benefit over selfishness.

Christian Parents Pray for Their Children

Worry changes nothing, but prayer changes everything—starting with our hearts. Prayer is a conversation with God where we can ask for our desires, listen to God, and thank HIM for who He is. It is also a time to intercede for the needs of our children, whether they are next to us or far away. Jesus set an example of prayer in his life, and he often went alone to pray because he knew that prayer is powerful. Philippians 4:6–7 says it beautifully: "Do not be anxious about anything, but in every situation, by prayer and petition, with thanksgiving, present your requests to God." As Christian parents, if a concern is on your heart, then God's ears are ready to listen and His power is accessible at any moment.

Christian Parents Protect Their Children

Our job is to equip our children with strong character and also to protect them both emotionally and physically. And if we want to safeguard our children, it is crucial to be aware of the influences, situations, and people that are affecting our children negatively. For example, you may notice a certain YouTube channel having an ill effect on your child, or perhaps your child is absorbing the behaviors of a friend with different morals. Regardless of the circumstance, Christian parents step in and create boundaries to protect their children when necessary.

Christian Parents Demonstrate Respect to Others

If we want our children to value respecting God and us, Christian parents must demonstrate respect to others. If we teach our children that they need to respect authority, but we talk negatively about our boss every day, we are sending a contradictory message about respect. My oldest son once witnessed someone yell at me and saw I was mad. My son leaned over and asked, "Are you wanting to say something mean right now?" I answered in a curt tone, "Yes, but I know it wouldn't be living out my faith." We laughed because he saw my conscious choice to show respect even though it wasn't easy. I believe those moments are what our children will remember when they are confronted with hardship, too.

Christian Parents are Present and Engaged

Psalm 145:18 tells us that "The Lord is *near* to all who call on him, to all who call on him in truth." This visual is everything to me because I want to know that when I need God, He is there. Similarly, Christian parents are emotionally near and ready to parent the needs of their children, whether that means playing with stuffed animals on the floor in imaginary voices or talking through scenarios of how to handle a difficult situation with friends. Christian parents stay engaged, knowing the frivolous conversation about Legos today will one day turn into a big conversation about life as a child grows.

The Challenges Christian Parents Face Today

I once said to a friend that "I wish I was raising my boys in an earlier generation because it would have been *so* much easier to protect them one hundred years ago." My friend then asked me if I would have enjoyed washing my sons' clothes by hand or making their bread from scratch. It was a good reminder that parenting has never been easy.

Parents in today's world face their own sets of challenges. Technology now requires us to be more attentive and engaged with our sons in ways parents of previous generations were not. Many parents inadvertently assume that as their son matures, they can loosen the reins and allow him to have less supervision. Unfortunately, the opposite is true. The things our sons are exposed to because of technology and social media often require more attention and guidance.

When a child is young, our job is often to protect them from physically hurting themselves. So we run ahead of them, moving furniture or objects that can cause them harm. Similarly, as our sons grow, our job is still to protect them—but now we are aiming to protect their minds and hearts. Following are some reasons why.

The Instantaneous World

One of the hidden challenges of raising children today is the fast-paced world in which we live in. Boston Digital, a digital marketing company, has defined a new demographic: "the impulse generation." This group is "is not an age-driven demographic; nor one confined by borders or languages" and is categorized by "short attention spans, high expectations, and demand for quick satisfaction." In other words, people no longer have to wait for anything, and this is the world our children are being raised in.

For example, few people visit the library anymore to do research in books, magazines, or encyclopedias. Instead, Google has your search results within seconds. Instant gratification. In 2015 Microsoft released a study saying the average human attention span had dropped to eight seconds, comparable to that of a goldfish.

Having patience is a virtue because it breeds a strong work ethic. Yet, when you're raised in an environment where all you want is instantly available, you can become less motivated to try hard when you are not getting the response you want. For example, a child who doesn't ace a test after studying for a mere 15 minutes may find that school isn't worth their time. When we understand this instant culture as a challenge, it can help us build patience in our sons by giving them opportunities to wait.

A General Decline in Religiosity

Jesus is alive and well, and His truths still set hearts free, but belief in these truths is declining in our children's generation. A Pew Research study found that only 49 percent of Millennials identify as Christian and the number of Americans who classify themselves as "religious nones" has grown by 30 million in the past decade. The COVID-19 pandemic, beginning in 2020, only continued this trend by breaking the habits of so many people who regularly attended church. Social distancing and stay-at-home safety measures made it difficult to physically attend, and some people felt as if it were no longer necessary.

To assume our children are living in a world with Christian values is no longer an accurate assumption. Instead, our children are growing up in a world where they are shown that having strong faith or morals doesn't necessarily add any positive value to someone's life. Unfortunately, that is being preached just as much or more than the idea that Jesus is the way, the truth, and the light, as John 14:6 teaches.

In a culture where anything goes and truth is subjective, teaching our children to stand on the firm truth of faith is life changing. As our children navigate this world, don't forget the power of giving them hope-filled and lifelong truth to lean on.

Video Games and Pseudo Realities

Gone are the days of video games like Tetris on an Atari or Pac-Man in an arcade. Today's video games have evolved into games that are so realistic and addictive, some children prefer to live in their alternate worlds rather than the real world of throwing a football with a friend. Although there are ways for children to join together and connect socially within these gaming consoles, there are also risks involved with that connection, too, including the ability for an adult with ill intent to be on the other side of the mic.

As parents raising our children in a culture of technology and gaming, it's important we remember that the human brain is like a sponge. Where our sons focus their time and energy will affect their emotions, mood, and behavior. It's important to consider if the video games we are allowing our sons to play seem violent, aggressive, and overly mature in content. Just as we want to protect their minds and hearts from harmful content in a movie or show, we also want to protect them from games that can expose them to unnecessary violence or negativity. You can easily protect your son by previewing any games you allow them to purchase.

Phones and Social Media

As I mentioned earlier, social media is an issue parents need to be aware of. Within the right boundaries, it can be a fun and effective way to connect with people, keep up with friends, and grow a business platform. But in the Netflix documentary *The Social Dilemma*, former social media employees from well-known tech companies like Google, Facebook, and Pinterest revealed how social media preys on its users through algorithms that manipulate a user's reality to keep them seeking affirmation from others and receiving one-sided views that align with their beliefs.

Additionally, social media is addictive and keeps our children's faces in their phones instead of focused on the faces in front of them, which often robs them from developing the social skills they need. Former design ethicist at Google Tristan Harris said, "We're training and conditioning a whole new generation of people that when we are uncomfortable or lonely or uncertain or afraid, we have a digital pacifier for ourselves that is kind of atrophying our own ability to deal with that." The more our children seek the likes and hearts they receive on their phone, the more it conditions them to seek approval from others.

Pornography

Pornography. If talking about this subject with your son makes you uneasy, you're not alone. But if you are raising boys, it is a word that needs to be defined and discussed within your home, and then safeguarded against because your son will likely be exposed to it before you know to ask. NetNanny.com reported that 11 is the average age for a boy to see pornography and shared that "technology company Bitdefender has reported children under the age of 10 now account for 22 percent of online porn consumption under 18 years old."

When I say pornography, I am not talking about your son seeing some innocent sex scene from a movie where two people are kissing and covered by sheets. Instead, I'm talking about your young son having the most explicit sexual scene you can imagine one click away from his tiny finger. Once a child is exposed to pornography, they often find themselves seeking it out repeatedly before understanding their own sexuality, which can cause confusion, shame, and pain. Pornography is something our boys are easily exposed to today and something Christian parents must be ready to face. I will dive into how to talk about this and safeguard against it in chapter 9 (page 86).

Raising a Christian Child in a Secular Society

As Christians, it can feel hard to know how to raise our children in a secular world but not allow them to absorb the influences of this world. Romans 12:2 says, "Do not conform to the pattern of this world, but be transformed by the renewing of your mind."

The Bible tells us not to be transformed by the world. But parents can easily feel confused in knowing the best way to do this. Does that mean keeping your children surrounded by people who have the same Biblical values? Or is it enough to teach their children these values and then send them into the world to share and live them? Families that desire to raise children with strong faiths can come to different conclusions in the best way to do this.

Some parents choose to put their children in public school, but others opt for a private Christian school or homeschooling. Some parents choose to have their children play on secular sports leagues, and some find a league that supports taking Sundays off. Some people try to only foster friendships with children from families that have similar beliefs, and some are okay to let their children be friends with people of differing faith backgrounds.

When we look around at different Christian families, we clearly see there is no one-size-fits-all mentality for raising Christian kids in a secular world. Instead, each family has to make decisions based on the personalities of their unique children, the circumstances around those children, and the resources within their family, and still maintain a flexible mindset regarding any decisions they make.

If reading this causes you to feel stressed over knowing what is right for your children, you can find comfort in knowing that a decision deemed good at one point in time can change down the road. And a decision made for one child may not be necessary for another.

For example, you can have two of your children spend time with a friend who doesn't believe in God. Over time, one of your children may end up inviting that friend to Sunday service, but your other child may end up telling you they don't believe in God anymore. Because every child and situation is unique, it's important for you to give yourself permission to have flexibility in your decision making.

If you are at a decision-making point for determining the right balance of secular versus Christian activities in your family, here are some questions to consider. As you discuss these questions and weigh the pros and cons, pray for discernment from God for what is best for your family. He desires to lead you and give wisdom.

- Does this activity have a benefit to my child?

- Is this activity convenient for our lives?

- Is this activity offered in a Christian environment?

- Does my child seem bothered by the outside influences they are seeing?

- Is my child still respecting my teachings more than the teachings they receive elsewhere?

- Does this friend influence my children negatively?

- Does my child have a positive influence on this friend?

- Does my child feel safe and protected?

After Jesus' resurrection, he returned to earth and shared these final words with the disciples in Matthew 28:19–20: "Then Jesus came to them and said, 'All authority in heaven and on earth has been given to me. Therefore, go and make disciples of all nations, baptizing them in the name of the Father and of the Son and of the Holy Spirit, and teaching them to obey everything I have commanded you.'" As parents raising children in a secular world, it's hopeful to remember that Jesus tells us to go in the world and influence it.

2

From Boys to Men: Your Child's Development

The pages ahead will overview your son's development by breaking down the influences that make your son who he is. They will then examine the parts of his life that affect his physical, emotional, and social development as he transitions into manhood. It can be a wild ride, but God is there by your side. Be sure to buckle up!

Major Influences on Your Child's Development

A few months ago, my oldest son and I were sitting next to each other on a plane when the flight attendant came by and asked me what I wanted to drink. I asked for a Diet Coke, and my son leaned over and asked me if he could get the same. The flight attendant and I both asked him if he would rather have a regular Coke. And then my son said something that I'll never forget: "Oh, I only knew there was diet. That's all I've ever seen my mom drink."

Yes, it was just a drink we were talking about, but this instance hit me straight in the heart. I could clearly see how much my life and my choices make a direct impact on my son's life as well.

When I tell this story, I'm always reminded of Proverbs 27:19: "As water reflects the face, so one's life reflects the heart." As I reflect on this Scripture, I have to ask myself, "What truths am I carrying in my heart, and am I okay for those beliefs rub off on my children?"

Let's take a deeper look and examine some of the primary influences that affect our sons' development.

His Unique Genetics

Nature or nurture. These opposing words battle against each other when people try to determine which has the biggest impact on raising a child. I have no way to prove one or the other, nor does anyone else, but I will forever believe that nature is a strong force to be reckoned with. All four of my sons have the same mom and dad, but they are profoundly different from one another.

My oldest son was such a light sleeper as a baby that if someone opened our garage door during his nap, he would hear it and wake up, causing me to dramatically question what I had done wrong to create such a light sleeper. My second son could sleep through anything, including his older brother screaming in the same room. Seeing the differences in the unique natures of my own sons is one reason I always encourage parents to consider their child's nature and how it affects their development. You get the credit for their nurture, but God gets the credit for their nature.

His Family System

You may be an individual, but you are also a son or a daughter, a sister or a brother, a niece or a nephew. Patterns within your family may involve marriage, divorce, depression, alcoholism, or a slew of other factors that influence your life in ways beyond your own comprehension. As a marriage and family therapist, I am trained to look at families as systems with members that profoundly—and subconsciously—influence one another, both emotionally and behaviorally.

Pioneering therapist Virginia Satir is revered for her theory that families should be viewed as "interdependent systems and imagined as hanging mobiles." One family member's movement or actions affects the other people on that mobile. Likewise, your son is greatly affected by the emotional patterns of functioning within your own family, immediate and extended. Yes, he's an individual with his own outside influences, but the family system he lives in holds a monumental influence on his daily life and choices.

His Family Values and Culture

All families have values that matter to them, whether spoken or not. Christian families likely have similar values based on the Bible, but they will also develop values based on their own families and cultures that affect their language, beliefs, and everyday habits from generation to generation.

When this Kansas girl moved to Texas at age 30, I didn't expect to meet so many people from Louisiana with Cajun roots and kind hearts who loved to cook gumbo for all occasions. They talked more quickly than the Kansans I grew up with and used their own unique phrasing and cadence. I'll never forget the day my three-year-old, who spent time in my neighbor's house, wanted to show me something and said in true Cajun form, "Come see, Mama." This experience is a good reminder of the power of cultural influence on our children.

His Community and Resources

Whether growing up on a farm in a small rural town, a home in modern-day suburbia, or an apartment in a city, your son will be exposed to unique messages from his environment about family structures, faith, finances, politics, leisure activities, and the value of education. As a result, the community around your son and the families within it will influence not only the life of your son, but also the future he believes is possible for himself.

As a Christian parent, it's helpful to have conversations with your son about what he experiences in his community and ask if he likes what he sees or if he feels called to a different path. It's also important that you do your best to expose him to different ways of life outside of your community and lifestyle so he can make wise decisions for his future.

His Friends

Friendships give our children a place to belong, but they also have influence over their lives. When I was little, I had never eaten a bologna sandwich until I went to my best friend's house. Soon after, I asked my mom to start buying bologna. Luckily, my friend's strong character, much finer than her cuisine choices, had a profound influence in my life, too.

The Bible talks about the upside and downside to friends starting in 1 Corinthians 15:33. "Do not be misled: 'Bad company corrupts good character.'" This verse serves as a strong warning: If your child is surrounded by bad friends, their character can be destroyed as a result. In contrast, we also learn in Proverbs 27:9 (TPT) that "sweet friendships refresh the soul and awaken our hearts with joy." So, whether our children receive positive or negative influence through friendship is all about the characters of the friends they have.

His School

Next to your home, there is no other environment your son will spend more time in throughout his childhood than his school. Although your child is learning about math, science, and reading, they are also learning about social norms, other cultures, varying household rules, and different ways of talking and acting.

For example, your son may not know that some children eat free or reduced-fee lunches until they meet a friend that does. Likewise, your son may eat free or reduced-fee lunches at school and discover that not everyone gets their midday meal at a lower price. School is a place where your child will learn a lot about economic, social, and cultural differences, so it's good to ask not only what they are learning academically, but also what they are learning socially.

His Extracurricular Activities

Extracurricular activities are great for health and well-being. Playing sports or playing instruments can boost a person's IQ by 10 percent, according to a study commissioned by DIY.com. In addition to igniting passion within our children, these activities also teach the value of having a good work ethic, the power of self-discipline, and the reward of being on a team.

If your child is struggling with finding positive influences, exploring activities and hobbies is an important place to start. On a middle school retreat, my youth leader had us spend one day with limited food available. We then went to serve the homeless community, where our experience engendered compassion for what it was like not to know when your next meal would be.

Spiritual Development

The spiritual development of our sons is important. Their ability to fully grasp who God is, and what He did for us through the sacrifice of His son, will likely not happen overnight. Instead, your son's faith will grow as he grows. It's your job to consistently feed him nuggets of truth in appropriate developmental doses, and at the same time know that God is the one who changes hearts. We just teach them.

Paul spoke about this exact concept with the Corinth church when he said, "I gave you milk, not solid food, for you were not yet ready for it." If Paul knew adults couldn't handle everything at once, we too need to remember this when teaching our children about faith.

Babies/Toddlers (0 to 3)

Intrinsically, toddlers are selfish (and adorable) little beings wired to get what they want while receiving love and giving love, too. The spiritual understanding of a toddler will center around how much God loves them. Incorporating simple habits into their daily life, like songs, short Bible stories with pictures, easy Scripture memory, and daily prayer, will introduce them to the presence of God and His love for them.

Early Childhood (ages 4 to 8)

Trying to teach little boys about Jesus can be tricky when they aren't mature enough to sit still. But remember, Jesus commends a childlike faith in Matthew 18 and compares it to the Kingdom of Heaven. (Don't take it personally if they ask to go fishing instead of wanting to listen about Jesus telling them to become fishers of men.)

For boys between the ages of four and eight, make the concept of faith alive, tangible, and helpful by telling Bible stories that are personal to their lives, asking probing questions, and praying with them on the spot in everyday moments in life.

Preteen (9 to 12)

As your son moves into the preteen years, his ability to read more Scripture, understand abstract spiritual concepts, and then apply these concepts to his life grows at its own rate and with your help.

For instance, you may finish reading about Jesus multiplying the fish and bread to feed the five thousand and then see your son unwilling to share a piece of his own bread with his sibling a few moments later. Instead of feeling frustrated, gently use the moment to help him make the connection. It is crucial we have grace with our sons so they stay interested in—not turned off by—faith.

Teen (13 to 18)

By the time your son is a teen, he likely is capable of reading the Bible on his own, having Bible discussion time with his family, and praying aloud. This doesn't mean he will want to, so it's important to find things that help him apply what he knows to his life and to foster habits that make an impact to him. One of my favorite questions to ask boys in this age range is, "How do you see God at work in your life?" He may or may not tell you something surprising, but it will give you an opportunity to hear your son's heart.

Emotional Development

We live in a world that tends to emphasize that girls are emotional and boys are more apathetic, but that belief couldn't be further from the truth. God created both girls *and* boys with emotions, and it's important that parents foster emotional intelligence—the ability to identify, understand, and process emotion—within their daughters and their sons. This is especially true during the adolescent years.

However, the prefrontal cortex, which controls the thinking and emotional reactions of teenage boys, is still developing. It doesn't mature in boys until their mid-20s. This means teens often rely on the more emotional and less advanced part of their brain, called the amygdala, to make decisions. As a result, some of the emotional changes they experience can feel challenging for their parents. Let's take a look at some of these below.

A Need for Independence

When a child is young, it seems you cannot even go to the bathroom without them desperately sticking their fingers under the crack of the door to try to reach you. There is *no* understanding of mine and yours; in the eyes of a toddler, everything is "ours" and centers around "our life together"—even your time in the bathroom.

Once your child enters the tween years, their need for independence will blossom. Many parents are taken aback when this occurs, but this emotional change is normal and should be celebrated. Your son is becoming his own person with unique thoughts and feelings, and he needs space to do it. Don't be surprised if one day you find a note on his door that says, "Knock before you enter."

Moodiness

Around the adolescent years, you may notice your son becoming emotional and moody. You may also find that you are the chosen person he unleashes his annoyance on.

This may feel maddening as he gets angry at you—until you notice a stream of tears running down his face, too. Within a span of 30 minutes, you may go from feeling like his least favorite person on the planet only to have him come and cuddle up next to you on the couch. His moods don't indicate he doesn't love you; they just indicate he is struggling with hormones and you are often the recipient of them.

Self-Consciousness

As your child's brain moves from being fully egocentric to aware of the emotions of others, he also begins to worry about what others think of him. As your son grows, he may no longer want you to hug him in front of his friends. He may start caring about whether what he is wearing is "cool" or how big his muscles are. All of a sudden, brand-name shirts and grooming become important.

These changes can feel frustrating, especially for your pocketbook, but they are developmentally normal. Your job is to remind him he is created by God with perfection and that he is fully loved and accepted through every phase.

Romantic Feelings

As hormones surge within your son, so might his feelings of romance and affection toward someone else. Your son may find himself thinking a certain someone in his math class is special. Don't be alarmed if you walk into his room one evening and find him listening to a sad love song. Then, as you sit down, he pours out his heart and tell you how much he thinks about this special someone but is scared to talk to them.

Many parents have strong feelings about the proper time to allow children to date and what those boundaries should be. (You'll learn more about this in chapter 16, page 120.) But it's important to remember that no matter your standard for dating, listening to your son's feelings and giving him a space to express himself allows you to remain a person he wants to confide in.

Pressure and Stress

As parents, it can seem like the only things our sons should be concerned with is getting fresh air, learning at school, and making friends. But even young children can feel stress. The CDC says approximately 7 percent of children aged 3 to 17 years (approximately 4.4 million) have diagnosed anxiety, and 3 percent of children aged 3 to 17 years (approximately 1.9 million) have diagnosed depression. These are growing at a faster rate, meaning this generation of children (and parents) is more anxious.

If your child is involved in sports or other extracurricular activities, be aware that the demands of multiple practices or rehearsals each week, plus tournaments or shows on the weekends, can be overwhelming. The activities can teach children a great work ethic and give them a place to focus their energy. Still, some children can end up feeling undue pressure and stress to perform well.

Genesis 1:27 says, "So God created mankind in his own image . . . male and female he created them." He then tells them to be fruitful and multiply and to rule over the animals of the earth. But we see no command that all men will love the color blue and all women will love to cook. Instead, we just see that both men and women were created in His image. The image of God the father.

If we want to have an accurate, healthy, and Godly definition of a man from the Bible, we can look to Jesus and his manhood. He was strong but also compassionate. He talked to men of society but also stood up for women and children. He was tough on calling out sin but tender with forgiveness. He cried the night before his crucifixion, yet didn't defend himself when the Roman guards were accusing him before Pilate. He was a combination of immense strength and incredible gentleness, and a "man" through it all.

Yet there is a subconscious and sad misconception interwoven throughout society that "real" men are tough. Stoic. Emotionless. Strong. Insensitive. Dominant. And innately superior to women. And that those traits, for all intents and purposes, combine to make the ultimate "man."

Think Gaston in *Beauty and the Beast* or Biff in *Back to the Future* or Anakin Skywalker in *Star Wars: Episode III*. These toxic males are the types of men that make you flinch because of their egocentric, narcissistic, and brazen ways; I throw up a little in my throat at the thought of interacting with one of them.

Yet for years, this archaic mindset of manhood, defined by the mythopoetic men's movement in the 1980s as "toxic masculinity," was a norm that was accepted by society but simultaneously hurt both men and women in its path. It did this by limiting a boy's definition of what it means to be a man and, thereby, contributing to the acceptance of destructive behaviors, including fighting, bullying, and abuse toward women.

Being masculine is not bad, and stereotypical masculine traits like being rough, tough, and wild can be parts of wonderful and Godly boys. It's also important for parents to understand there is not one single definition of what it means to be a man. As a parent, you may have one son who loves to spit, climb trees, and wrestle, and another son who likes to draw, sing, and play imaginary games. Both of these types of boys are created by God and in His image. (You also find girls that fit both scenarios, too.)

So, as we seek to raise strong boys to love the Lord, it's important to remember there is not a one-size-fits-all type of masculinity. Instead, it's about teaching our sons to be Christ-like as they boldly grow into the unique men God made them to be.

Social Development

In the Bible, you quickly learn that humans are hardwired for connection. Jesus chose 12 disciples to do His ministry with because He knew that we are created as social beings and thrive when living life with others. (Introverts, that includes you!) Yet, if you ask anyone to name a hard time in life, often the middle school years are mentioned because children have to manage their social interactions as they deal with so many bodily changes.

And the result can often be awkward memories of food getting stuck in your braces over lunch or getting picked on because your feet were too big for your body when you were 12 years old. As parents, it's important to be keyed to the social challenges our children are experiencing during this age so we can be equipped to support them through it.

Need to Belong Outside of Home

Between the late grade school to early middle school years, social interactions outside of your home become important to your son. Mom and Dad are no longer the heroes, and even though children know they have a place to hang out and socialize at home, they no longer seem to be as content just hanging out with family on a Friday night. Instead, they begin to feel a desire to connect more with friends and be a part of a bigger group.

If you live in a neighborhood where children play outside together, you may notice your son wanting to hang out more with local friends. Or, if your son has a phone at this age, you may notice him texting friends more. Or, if he likes to game, you may notice him asking to hop on and play with a friend. This transition can sometimes hurt parents when their kids no longer want to just hang out at home, but these changes are developmentally appropriate and should be welcomed.

Peer Pressure

If I asked you what phrase best defines being a young teen, peer pressure would surely be on the list. We all know that it affects our everyday life (even as adults) and certainly becomes a focus as children begin launching into adolescence. But not all peer pressure is bad. It's all about the type of friends your children keep.

Some friends might pressure your son into going to church, but others may tell them cussing is cool and introduce them to sexual concepts you never wanted them to know. It's important to understand how strong the desire to fit in can be and how hard it can feel for kids to go against the grain. As the ones here to protect them, it's important to equip our sons with tools for saying no, and to monitor the influences they have around them as they grow in their ability to make wise decisions.

A Fear of Rejection

One of the greatest social fears of children in the preteen years is fear of rejection. Some children seem to fit in no matter where they go, but other children may struggle to fit anywhere. If they are taught to be themselves, yet are picked on or overlooked, it can be a hard road to navigate. Even children with the strongest spirits can struggle when the thing that made them cool when they were young—like their long hair—is suddenly rejected by other students at their school.

As parents, it is important to be sensitive to this struggle within children. If you sense that your child is experiencing rejection from peers, it is important to teach them about the character that can come from these times, and at the same time show empathy for the pain of the experience. It is also wise for parents to help children seek out hobbies that allow them to find acceptance in positive ways.

Independent Thinking

When children are little, they willingly embrace the ideals you teach them. Even if they are prone to asking why, they often accept your answer with certainty. Take this common interchange as an example:

Them: Why can't I swallow gum?

Us: Because it gets stuck in your stomach.

Them: Weird, but okay.

But as children grow, they may no longer want to embrace norms you taught them; instead, they'll begin experimenting with new ideas and decisions that may surprise you. One day they may be vegan, another a declared libertarian, and another unsure of the faith you are teaching.

It can be tempting to tell them the right way to think, but wise parents ask questions, listen with an open heart, and give room for their child to grow in wisdom. God gives us room to choose Him, so we have to give our children room, too.

A Desire to Make a Mark

Some children may surprise you; instead of desiring to fit in, they may want to stand out. They don't just want to be in a band, they want to lead the band and do it in all black with a mohawk and leather vest. As you watch them display their bold spirit, you may wonder if you are raising them to have too much confidence, especially as they buck the traditional system and turn heads while doing it.

But never forget that God uses all personalities, including strong spirits, for his good plans, and it's important to remember that not all children will be quiet, submissive, and conventional. God loves variety, and we should celebrate that, too. Your job as the parent is to find ways to let your trailblazer make a mark but still stay safe. This can be a delicate balance of prayer and love to parent well. But God desires to give you wisdom and guide you.

Celebrating Your Son's Authentic Self

When we open our Bibles as parents, we see that Scripture teaches us that each of our children is uniquely created by God. Then, Ephesians 2:10 (ESV) also shares a similar message, stating, "For we are his workmanship, created in Christ Jesus for good works, which God prepared beforehand, that we should walk in them."

As parents, it's easy to read this Scripture and confidently encourage our sons to celebrate the parts of themselves that are different from others, until that same son comes home and tells us that someone made fun of them for liking art classes more than sports.

Moments like these are pivotal times, when teaching our sons to celebrate their authentic selves becomes more important than ever. Based on what the Bible teaches us, that every person is God's unique workmanship, here are some practical ways to do just that:

- Sit down and have your son make a list of the unique gifts God has given them, and have them thank God for those gifts.

- Challenge them to consider how their gifts are similar to or different from their friends' and family's.

- Ask them, "What are reasons God gives us different gifts?"

- As parents, share ways God has used your unique gifts for good throughout your lives. Then, challenge your son to ponder what "good works" God might use their unique traits for.

Physical and Sexual Development

Puberty is a word that has made tweens blush with embarrassment for generations. But despite the awkward feelings that often surround it, puberty is truly a unique and memorable time in life created by God, when our boys become young men before our eyes. I mean, even Jesus went through puberty!

Boys begin to mature between the ages of 9 and 15, usually around 12 years old. That's when the pituitary gland starts making two hormones, causing the testicles to grow and produce testosterone. Puberty is the time in your son's life when he will grow at the fastest rate ever, second only to his infancy.

If you have a boy in this age range, it is vital you take time to talk to him about puberty before he begins experiencing it himself. Because he will hear about it somewhere, and it's important that information comes from you first.

Physical Changes

During puberty, your son's testosterone levels will peak, causing him to undergo a variety of physical changes, including the ones we are all accustomed to seeing and hearing in boys—such as those infamous voice cracks. The first step in puberty begins with the enlargement of your son's scrotum and testes. A growth spurt typically follows within a year, as well as enlargement of their penis in both length and width. And you may notice your son suddenly becoming prouder of this region of his body, so don't be surprised.

During this time, hair growth increases on his face, chest, armpits, back, and pubic area. You will hear cracks in his voice, and his voice will deepen. His arms, legs, hands, and feet will grow faster than the rest of his body. He may also notice his shoulders broadening and find more muscle mass in his body. Some young men will also notice a slight enlargement of their breasts, called gynecomastia, which normally goes away within a few years. Your son's face will also become oilier, and he may develop some acne and need to wear deodorant. If he doesn't notice that change, help him out by leaving deodorant for him on the bathroom counter. His teachers and friends will thank you.

Sexual Changes

In addition to physical changes, your son will experience a variety of sexual changes during puberty as well. Remember that God created all of us to sexually mature, so it is important that you are comfortable with this new phase of child-rearing and remember it is something God created as good! (So no giggles, parents!)

If you've changed a little boy's diaper, you've likely noticed that even infants can have erections. During puberty, your son will begin to have erections as a response to sexual excitement, in addition to spontaneous erections for no reason at all. Sometimes these erections will result in ejaculation, and some boys may wake up realizing they ejaculated while sleeping, also known as a "wet dream."

After discovering their penises, many young boys have fondled themselves because it feels good, but once puberty happens, many adolescent boys become curious about masturbation and may begin asking questions as to if this is a normal thing. Additionally, you may notice they are suddenly much more interested in being around someone they like and touching, hugging, or even talking about kissing them. Therefore, it is crucial as parents that you are the ones teaching and training them about their bodies, and showing love and comfort toward these normal changes is important.

The Look of a Changing Relationship

We all know that part of parenting is watching our children grow up, because they can't stay little forever, and we shouldn't expect them to. As the years pass and you watch your growing boy leave with friends for a Friday night football game, you may find yourself missing the little boy who used to cuddle up in your lap for a weekend movie.

Does he even need me anymore? You may wonder. The answer to that question will always be yes! Your son will always need you, but he will just begin to need you in different ways as the years pass. It's our job as parents to figure out what those needs are so we can guide our sons as they grow.

When your son was young, he may have cried out "Mommmmmmmmmy!" when he hurt his knee, clearly signaling he needed you (and a Band-Aid). But as he grows, instead of crying when he's hurt, he may tell you to leave him alone and shut the door in your face, leaving you feeling confused and rejected.

But in those moments, it's important to remember your son needs you no less. He just shows his needs differently. So, your job as he grows from babyhood to manhood is to figure out how to love him best and at the same time point him to Christ and remind him of God's great plans for his life.

The Bible says in Luke 2:52 that Jesus grew in "wisdom and stature and in favor with God and man," and that is the same goal we should have for our sons—to help them grow physically, mentally, and spiritually. We do this by showing them love when they act like they need it—and also when they act like they don't need it.

3

Defining Your Values and Goals

I n the chapter ahead, I will discuss what traits make for Godly character in boys and use that discussion to help you reflect on which of those traits matter most to you as a parent. As we close, I will challenge you to create specific parenting goals centered around raising boys with the traits you identified.

Raising a Man of Christian Character

When my second son was in first grade, he threw up in the school hallway. No one saw him, so he walked to the bathroom, got a paper towel, and started cleaning it up until his teacher walked over and stopped him. When she called to tell me about the incident, she said, "And I just had to tell you that I've never seen a first grader with such strong character to clean up his own puke. Good job, Mama."

It was a funny instance (that of course made me tear up, too) because it was something my son did on his own. I never taught him that he needed to clean up his own puke—he just didn't know janitors did that for you. But I did use that instance to talk to all of my sons about character and how much people notice it.

When I consider the word "character," I naturally pair it with the word "good," but character is individually distinctive, which means it's up to us as parents to teach *good* character to our children.

Throughout the Bible, we see that good character is a value to be praised, and Ruth, David, and Job are recognized for having it. Their stories teach us that Godly character is the demonstration of Jesus's teachings at work in our lives. Galatians 5:22–23 defines it well: "But the fruit of the Spirit is love, joy, peace, forbearance, kindness, goodness, faithfulness, gentleness and self-control. Against such things there is no law."

As parents, we often assume we are teaching our children strong character without taking time to reflect on these traits with our sons. We need to be clear about character traits that matter to us and ensure that our sons are familiar with the traits that make for strong character, too. Let's take a look at those here.

Respect

Boys with Godly character show respect to others because they understand that choosing to respect others honors God and elicits respect in return. Nehemiah, who was working as the cupbearer to King Artaxerxes, found out that the wall around Jerusalem had been destroyed. He really wanted to go back to Jerusalem and rebuild the wall, but he knew he needed permission first. So he took the time to ask the king in Nehemiah 2:5: "If it pleases the king . . . let him send me to the city in Judah where my ancestors are buried so that I can rebuild it." The king granted him permission because he respected him.

Integrity

Integrity is a trait that is best described as being honorable in your words and actions when someone is watching and when someone is not. It's the little boy who only takes two pieces of candy when the Halloween bowl has no one next to it. The Bible says in Psalm 78:72 that God chose David to shepherd his people, and he did so with "integrity of heart." Because David was described as a man after God's own heart, I can't help but believe the integrity of our hearts matters to God.

Humility

The Bible is full of passages about humility, so it's an important value to teach our sons. One reason I love the Christian faith is because it flips the script on how humans gain success and favor with God. Jesus tells us to get at the back of the line if we want to be first, to love our neighbor as ourselves, and that the meek people shall inherit the earth, not the bossy, powerful, and cutthroat ones. It's tiring to live a life always seeking to elevate your status, so Godly boys need to know that God desires to see their humility.

Compassion

As we discussed in chapter 1 (page 2), God describes himself as compassionate toward us; therefore, as parents, we want to be compassionate to our children, and we also want our children to live out compassion in their own lives. I always remind my sons that none of us choose the family or circumstance we are born into. Instead, God does. Because of this, we should have compassion for all the types of people walking this earth that may have a harder or easier road than us. But we do get to choose how we treat those around us.

Kindness

In a similar manner to compassion, the Bible always tells us that God is kind and that His immense kindness leads us to repentance. Kindness is powerful because it compels others to behave differently in response to it. Therefore, Godly character involves kindness in our sons. One of my favorite quotes is "Be kind. For everyone you meet is fighting a hard battle." I love this because we often have no idea what someone else is experiencing, but we can make sure that in the midst of their battle, they experience kindness from us.

Leadership and Autonomy

Every day as my sons leave, I say, "Be a leader," because to have Godly character, you have to be okay to lead yourself closer to Christ. Sometimes that means walking away from the crowd and standing on your own. Having a leadership quality doesn't mean you will be a leader on a stage or a leader of a company, it means you know who your ultimate leader is, and at the end of the day, you stand by God and trust Him to lead your life over the approval of others.

Service-Minded

The Bible tells us that Jesus came to the earth not for us to serve him but for him to serve others. In response to this truth, Godly boys serve others, because when our sons have a humble heart, their eyes are opened to the world around them. Instead of seeking to serve themselves, they see the world full of other humans created by God. When you see the world through this lens, your heart no longer sees everything as me against the world, but instead a world that can be changed by your service.

Honesty

I often tell my sons, "Godly boys tell the truth when it's easy, but the strongest Godly boys tell the truth even when it's hard." When I think about the things most important to God, I think of the Ten Commandments, which are the values God thought were important enough to give to Moses to share with the Israelites in the desert. In those commandments, we see these words, "You shall not give false testimony about your neighbor." In other words, speak truth. In a world where truth is subjective to many, a person who is honest in words and action matters more than ever.

Hard Work

I have a phrase: "Lazy doesn't get you far." When I say it, my boys know I mean, "Get your little booty up off that couch" or "Get ready to dust and mop." God actually gives us a day of rest in the Sabbath. But he also tells us to do everything as if we are doing it for *Him*. Proverbs 10:4 says, "Lazy hands make for poverty, but diligent hands bring wealth." Although wealth is not the goal in life, we will never know how God desires to use us if we don't get up and offer our lives to Him.

Self-Control and Accountability

Godly boys understand that their actions matter, and Titus 2:6 tells adults to encourage them to show self-control. But when our sons do mess up, they take responsibility for the things they've done, apologizing when necessary. Even though accountability can be hard, the more our children understand that we are all prone to sin and mistakes, the easier it is to accept responsibility, knowing those mistakes don't define them. Instead, Jesus's forgiveness does. In order to walk in that forgiveness and grace, our sons must accept their own actions, first knowing Godly boys won't live a life with no mistakes. Instead, they will know how to admit and apologize for the ones they make.

WHAT DO YOU VALUE THE MOST?

We just discussed a variety of traits that make for Godly character in our sons. 1 Corinthians 12:27 tells us that "Now you are the body of Christ, and each of you is a part of it"—it's up to you to reflect on the traits that matter most to you as a parent. Here are some questions to consider when thinking about what you desire to see in your sons.

- When your son leaves your house, what traits do you most desire for him to walk away with?

- If your son's teacher or coach was describing him, what traits would you most want to be on that list?

- What traits did your parents instill in you as a child? Which of these traits have contributed to your success in life, and which have been a struggle for you?

Evaluating Your Parenting Goals

Now that you've had some time to focus on what character traits matter most to you, it is now important to widen the scope and consider the parenting goals you need to create to support the traits being strengthened and developed within your son.

Because Christian parents are intentional, they don't assume that just wanting their kids to have strong, Godly character is enough. Instead, they take time to create goals that build character traits like honesty, service, and self-control that they desire to see within their sons.

In order to develop my specific parenting goals, I like to think of my sons coming home to visit me in their late 20s, all sitting around the dinner table eating a meal and talking about their lives. Then I ask myself, "What types of conversations do I hope to hear from them, and what traits do I want them to possess as grown men?"

From there, I work my way backward to think through tangible goals I need to set that will make those traits come to life. This thought process can be as simple as, *I hope that once we finish the meal, they would all jump in and help clean the kitchen.* (And I hope their ability to clean up after themselves makes their future spouses happy, too.) So if that's a future goal, then I would set a current goal of teaching them to carry their plates to the sink to wash them today.

Below are some universal goals of Christian parents for you to consider that can help you create more specific goals for your son later. These goals lay a foundation for your parenting as you apply more targeted parenting strategies that are discussed in parts 2 (page 49) and 3 (page 85).

Universal Parenting Goals

No matter who you are or how your family functions, I want to offer some general goals that can be helpful for all Christian families that are seeking to create men of God. As you read through them, consider what specific goals might need to be added to meet the needs of your child.

To raise sons that have a personal relationship with Jesus.
As Christian parents, our goal in teaching our children about Jesus is introducing them to a relationship with their personal savior that can be their hope, joy, and strength through the ups and downs of life. We cannot make life perfect for our children, but we can introduce them to God's perfect love for them that will never leave them as they grow. My prayer for my children and yours is that this Scripture (Psalm 76:26) becomes their life experience: "My flesh and my heart may fail, but God is the strength of my heart and my portion forever."

To raise sons with strong and secure relationships with their parents and family.
Our family is the first place our sons get to receive love and learn how to love others. The Bible tells us to honor our father and mother in the Ten Commandments, and many verses continue this same sentiment, but 1 John 4:20 takes it a step further and says: "Whoever claims to love God yet hates a brother or sister is a liar. For whoever does not love their brother and sister, whom they have seen, cannot love God, whom they have not seen." Our family can be the easiest place to treat others poorly, but the greatest place to live out our faith consistently.

To raise sons that know Scripture.
We want our sons to believe in God, but we also want them to know the character of God, and we get to know His character by reading His Word from Genesis to Revelations. I have done Bible studies my whole life and had always loved Scripture, but I had

never read the Bible from start to finish until three years ago. I knew doing it was powerful, but after reading the whole thing, I realized my faith and trust in God's plan for my life had grown exponentially. Teaching our sons to love Scripture is one of the most powerful tools for their hearts and minds.

To raise sons who love and serve others as Christ would.
If we are raising sons to love Jesus, then we are also raising sons to love others. Matthew 23:11 says, "The greatest among you will be your servant," and Jesus himself says that he came to serve others. The Bible talks about caring for the widows, the orphans, and the poor throughout all of Scripture, so it's hard to say your faith is strong without demonstrating this belief in your life. Teaching a son to serve others does not mean they do not value themselves; but instead it means they know their immense value from God and, as a result, are compelled to serve others.

To raise sons with a healthy thought and heart life.
Spiritually healthy sons are emotionally and mentally healthy sons, too. If we truly are filled with the Holy Spirit and embrace who God tells us to be, then we know how much our heart and thoughts matter. Proverbs 4:23 says, "Above all else, guard your heart, for everything you do flows from it." And we guard our hearts by intentionally guarding our thoughts. Philippians 4:8 tells us how: "Finally, brothers and sisters, whatever is true, whatever is noble . . . whatever is admirable—if anything is excellent or praiseworthy—think about such things." Godly parents help their sons keep a healthy thought life.

To raise sons with confidence and a strong sense of self-worth in Christ.
If your son looks to the world for approval, he may find that one day the world says he's the homecoming king and the next day he's getting picked on at lunch. This happens because the world is moody and full of lies and emotions that shift with trends. In the book *The Good and Beautiful God,* author James Bryan

Smith says that as believers in Christ, we see our identity as "one in whom Christ dwells." When a child knows this, he can step away from seeking the approval of man and seek the approval of God first.

To raise sons with a strong work ethic and Kingdom purpose. One of my favorite Bible verses is Jeremiah 29:11, which teaches us that God has plans for our life that are to prosper us and give us a future and hope. When we pair this teaching with Colossians 3:23–24, which says, "Whatever you do, work at it with all your heart, as working for the Lord, not for human masters, since you know that you will receive an inheritance from the Lord as a reward," we can teach our sons to find great purpose in even the most monotonous of tasks, believing God can use them for more than what the world sees.

WHAT ARE YOUR OWN PARENTING GOALS?

Now that you've had time to reflect on the character traits that matter most to you and consider some broad parenting goals, it's time to get specific in your own life and determine what matters most to you as a parent and what specific goals you need to create to make that happen. As you set goals for yourself, here are some questions for you to consider:

- What traits are most important to me?

- Would my son know the traits I just listed are important in our home?

- Have these words been defined to him?

- How am I helping promote these traits in my home?

- Am I exhibiting habits in my own life that I do not want my children to have?

- Likewise, am I demonstrating habits I want my son to mimic?

- Am I happy with the spiritual example I am setting?

- Do I like the example I am setting in physical health and eating?

PART TWO

Foundational Parenting Principles

In the next five chapters, we are going to dive into foundational parenting principles for every Christian parent. The principles will focus on creating a healthy groundwork between you and your son so that more specific tactics in part 3 (page 85) will become more effective.

4

Establishing a Foundation of Love and Trust

There's a quote by George Eliot that says, "Life began by waking up and loving my mother's face." (Please insert "father's face" if you are the dad reading.) As a mother of four little boys, this quote has always touched my heart because I want my sons to always find comfort in my face, no matter how weathered or wrinkled it may grow.

But even more than that, I love this quote because of the truth it speaks—what a parent's love really does for a child. We are our child's first understanding of tangible love on this earth, and everything we demonstrate to them from birth either teaches them to feel loved or it doesn't. This means our example of love in our children's lives has a profound effect on them.

The Bible defines love in 1 Corinthians as a list of qualities that demonstrate what love in action looks like. And as Christian parents who desire for our children to know God's love, we must not just say we love them, but we must also demonstrate this type of love to our sons.

"Love is patient, love is kind. It does not envy, it does not boast, it is not proud. It does not dishonor others, it is not self-seeking, it is not easily angered, it keeps no record of wrongs.

Love does not delight in evil but rejoices with the truth. It always protects, always trusts, always hopes, always perseveres. Love never fails." 1 Corinthians 13:4–8

When we live out this type of Godly love to our children, our children will trust and connect with us and others well. According to psychiatrist and attachment theory pioneer Dr. John Bowlby, when caregivers are available, responsive, and accessible, children are able to have healthy connections in relationships and a strong sense of self.

Although many assume that being too available to our children can create needy and dependent kids, Bowlby's research found the opposite. Secure attachment and connection with caregivers at a young age is what fosters independence and autonomy in adulthood. Additionally, secure attachment sets up our children for healthy relationships—including their relationship with God.

Likewise, a child raised in an abusive home or with parents who are disconnected or harsh may struggle to connect with the Heavenly Father, due to projecting their experience of human love onto Him. It's also wise to note that if you as a parent came from an abusive or troubled home, you may also struggle to show love and trust in relationships. Taking time to address this as a parent will be invaluable as you seek to raise kids with a healthy sense of love and trust in their lives.

Practical Pointers

There's a quote by George MacDonald that says, "To be trusted is a greater compliment than being loved." But in order to raise kids who trust us and connect with us, we must love them well and consistently. Because no one cares to accept influence from someone who doesn't make them feel loved.

When I was a little girl, I realized that if I woke up in the middle of the night and called out my mom's name, she would come to my room without hesitation. One night I decided to put her to the test and called out to her as softly as I could because I wanted to see if she could hear me no matter what. To my amazement, within a few moments, my mom was in my room. Parents don't need superhuman hearing to create trust, but they can make God's love tangible when they love their children well.

So, let's explore some ways to create trust in our homes.

5 Tips for Creating Strong Trust and Healthy Attachment

1. **Be available and accessible in a consistent manner for both physical and emotional needs.** Secure attachment is built when we consistently meet our children's emotional and physical needs without question. A parent who shows up to watch a ball game but doesn't ask the child how they feel after the ball game is only showing up for half of their needs. Chapter 11 (page 96), discusses how to connect emotionally with your child.

2. **Let your words match your actions.** The old adage "Actions speak louder than words" has a lot of truth in life. When actions match your words, trust is built because children quickly learn you have integrity and can be counted on. Follow through on the little things like kissing them good night before bed so they know you will do the same for the big things, too.

3. **Apologize if you mess up, and forgive them when they make mistakes.** As parents, we make mistakes, and it's important that our children see us admit when we mess up and forgive them when they mess up, too. This shows our children that we know we aren't perfect and also need God's grace.

4. **Take steps to repair trust when it's broken.** In his book *The Four Laws of Love*, Jimmy Evans says that "trust is earned in droplets but lost in buckets." In parenting, there are times

when you might break your son's trust because of something simple, like running late to a game, or something more serious, like hurt from divorce. Whatever the scenario, here are some simple steps to rebuild trust:

- Acknowledge to your child that you made a mistake.

- Ask your son to tell you how they feel about it.

- Apologize for the mistake that was made.

- Ask your child what you can do to rebuild trust.

5. **Love your son in his love language.** In his book *The Five Love Languages*, Dr. Gary Chapman teaches that there are five languages in which people receive love, including physical touch, words of affirmation, quality time, acts of service, and gifts. Just like adults, children also have ways in which they receive love more effectively. Learning your child's love language, and then learning to be intentional in showing love, can save you time and energy and also build a strong connection with your child.

A Quick Test for Identifying Your Son's Love Language

ASK HIM:

- Do you feel most loved when I say "I love you?" (Words of Affirmation)

- Do you feel most loved when I hug and cuddle you? (Physical Touch)

- Do you feel most loved when I take you to your practice and help you put your clothes away? (Acts of Service)

- Do you feel most loved when I surprise you with a donut or new shirt from the store? (Gifts)

- Do you feel most loved when we hang out together and play games? (Quality Time)

What's the Word?

In Genesis 22, God tells Abraham, the patriarch of God's chosen people, to take his only son, Isaac, his child of promise given in old age, and carry him up Mt. Moriah to sacrifice him to God, a foreshadowing of God's ultimate sacrifice of His only son for us.

I can only imagine what was going through Abraham's and Isaac's minds as they were walking up the mountain, preparing to make a sacrifice. After Abraham gave the wood to Isaac, Isaac even asks his father in verse 7, "The fire and wood are here," Isaac said, "but where is the lamb for the burnt offering?" Abraham answered, "God himself will provide the lamb for the burnt offering, my son." And the two of them went on together.

When I read this story, I have to assume that Isaac must have wondered if he was the sacrifice. Scholars say he was actually not a child but around the age of thirty-seven in this story. Yet he continued to trust his father. Abraham got so far as to lift his knife to sacrifice Isaac, only for an angel to stop him and say it was only to test Abraham's heart. Then, God provided a ram from the bushes for sacrifice instead.

As hard as this story can be to read, it's a huge story of trust. First, God wanted to test Abraham to see if he was trustworthy as the father of God's chosen people. Then, Abraham trusted God so deeply that he was willing to sacrifice his own son. Finally, Isaac trusted his father so immensely that he did not run away. Yet, God loved them so much; He provided what they needed without anything happening to Isaac. This story exemplifies how strong relationships and faith center around love and trust.

I will never forget the day I forgot my oldest son at school. His two younger brothers were napping, and I somehow lost track of time. When I frantically screeched up to the school, he was the last one sitting on the school steps, alone. I was ready for him to get in the van and ask why I had forgotten him, but instead he said, "I knew you were coming, but I was wondering what you were doing!"

His words touched my heart because they showed me how much he trusted me to be there. They reminded me that deep-rooted trust is a goal of Godly parenting because it gives us a foundation to teach our children's hearts about God's love, too.

As we close out this chapter, I want to remind you that if you ever find yourself at a loss in your parenting, please remember that love covers the pain of other issues; as Proverbs 10:12 states: "Hatred stirs up conflict, but love covers over all wrongs."

And as 1 Corinthians 13:1–2 teaches us, love behind our actions produces trust, so let's always love boldly. "If I speak in the tongues of men or of angels, but do not have love, I am only a resounding gong or a clanging cymbal. If I have the gift of prophecy and can fathom all mysteries and all knowledge, and if I have a faith that can move mountains, but do not have love, I am nothing."

FOR REFLECTION:

- Do I know my child's love language, and am I taking steps to love them with intention?

- Is there any past hurt in our relationship that I need to acknowledge and address?

- Do I have hidden hurt from my past that is preventing me from loving my child as the Bible teaches?

- Have I broken the trust of my children, and do I need to seek repair?

5

Modeling Your Values

My sister and I both received our bachelor's degrees from Kansas State University, so naturally after graduating, we both dreamed that our children would one day want to attend there, too.

However, once I graduated from K-State and moved to Texas, I really only mentioned K-State's name to my sons when I was watching a football game here or there or telling an old college story, since my husband was raised a Nebraska fan.

My sister, on the other hand, married a man from a family legacy of K-State fans, so her sons have been raised with K-State memorabilia around their house, K-State shirts in every size, and watching K-State play every game. Not surprisingly, her son proclaims that he wants to attend K-State when he's older, and my sons are leaning toward attending a Texas university.

But I have no doubt that if I had spent my life showing as much passion for K-State as my sister and brother-in-law had, my sons would also feel inclined to attend the school, too, because our children follow our lead in their passions.

This concept makes me think of my favorite parenting verse of all time from Deuteronomy 6:4–9, which reads,

"Hear, O Israel: The Lord our God, the Lord is one. Love the Lord your God with all your heart and with all your soul and with all your strength. These commandments that I give you today are to be on your hearts. Impress them on your children. Talk about them when you sit at

home and when you walk along the road, when you lie down and when you get up. Tie them as symbols on your hands and bind them on your foreheads. Write them on the doorframes of your houses and on your gates."

I love this verse because it shows that when we love something, we don't keep it to ourselves. And we don't want to. Instead, when we love something, much like a sports team—we talk about it. We write about it. We keep things that remind us about it near us. We even wear things that show our dedication to it, not just when our team plays a game, but year-round.

Likewise, when we believe in God and his commandments, as Christian parents, it's our job to model the values and teachings that we believe. And not just once or twice. Or here or there. But every day. In all the ways. We have to practice what we preach, knowing that this example makes a profound impact on the growing faith of our children.

Practical Pointers

Earlier, I listed qualities God shows to us in His parenting of us. We have also talked about the traits that we want to help our children develop, including respect, leadership, and autonomy, and how to establish and encourage a foundation of love.

As Christian parents seeking to show how much these traits matter, not just in raising our sons but in our own lives as well, we have to make it a priority to figure out where we are doing well and where we have room to grow. We also have to evaluate where we are emotionally and mentally, and make sure we take action when we know we are struggling. Our own mental health affects the well-being of our children.

Ways to Model Spiritual and Emotional Health in Front of Your Children:

- Take time with God and His Word each day, and let your children see it or join in.

- Engage in some kind of church or faith community group. Share how it impacts you.

- Create space for self-care, including exercise, reading, coffee with a friend, etc. (It's okay to vocalize to your children that those small habits allow you to give your best to them.)

- Attend therapy or talk to someone if you are struggling emotionally.

- Take time to pray alone and with your family.

- Identify and eliminate unnecessary habits that disturb your peace and raise anxiety.

- Limit unnecessary media intake. (It's just as bad for adults as it is for our children.)

- Avoid angry or heated conversations toward children or others until you are calm.

How to Model What You Believe:
As mentioned in chapter 1 (page 2), Christian parents are intentional. We can be intentional by taking time to have meaningful conversations with our children about what's in their hearts, since the Bible teaches us how valuable the heart is in forming character. Therefore, intentional conversations with our children should be the norm, not the exception.

Try starting the conversation:
"Hi, son. As you know, helping you grow in your faith and character is important to me, and that starts with me and what I teach you. So today, I want to give you a chance to ask me questions and

talk to me about what you're learning from me. When I teach you about the Bible, I am also teaching you about the things I value."

Questions to Ask:

- Do you see that my faith is important to me?

- What values do you see as important to me? (Please note: Depending on the age of your son, you might need to define what those values are and then let them process those before answering.)

- Where do you think I do a good job of showing you that faith matters?

- How do you see me living out this trait?

- Where do my actions cause confusion in what I am teaching you?

- In what ways am I not living out what I am teaching you? (For younger children you might just ask, "What do I do that you do not like?")

Tips for Making This Productive:
Parents, when taking time to engage with the heart of your son, please listen to your child's interpretation of their experience with you and avoid defensiveness. When we ask how people experience and feel about us, there is no right or wrong answer. Listen to what your child feels, and then respond accordingly with love, gentleness, and compassion.

Additionally, remember that your child is actually a perfect person to learn and grow from, too, because they see you in your most vulnerable environment.

What's the Word?

It's a running joke in church that if a Sunday school teacher or preacher asks a question, your safe-bet answer is always Jesus. But an example of what it looks like to model your values before your children, there is nowhere better to look than Jesus. His teachings were not always easy, but He didn't say what He wasn't willing to do. That is our model in how to best show others the Christian way.

For example, Jesus taught his followers all about humility and serving others. To demonstrate this concept, in His final meal with the disciples before his death, He washed their feet and then said these words in John 13:15: "I have set you an example that you should do as I have done for you." Because He knew that telling others to serve others is a lot easier if they see their leader doing it first. Likewise, the most compelling example for teaching children how powerful faith in action can be is seeing their parent live out their faith when it's hard.

Several years ago, when my husband and I were still in college, we were driving in downtown Kansas City with my dad in an area with many homeless people. When waiting at a light, a staggering man came up to my dad's window asking for money, and without a thought, my dad rolled down his window and gave him money. My husband asked, "But what happens if he takes the money and uses it for alcohol?" My dad answered, "My job isn't to judge what he does with it. I'm just told to give to the poor." My husband still credits that as a memory that brought him to a close relationship with God. Because he saw my dad live out his faith instead of just speak it.

In this chapter, I have highlighted the importance of modeling the faith you believe and speak about to your children. Just as telling our children to eat healthy and then serving them ice cream and cake for dinner is counterproductive, telling our sons to have certain character traits without modeling those same traits is also confusing and contradicting. They don't know which way is right, and because their desire is to follow our lead, as parents we must be consistent in what we live before them.

The Bible is full of passages that talk about imitating God, including Ephesians 5:1 (NASB), "Therefore be imitators of God, as beloved children," and Hebrews 13:7 (NASB), "Remember those who led you, who spoke the word of God to you; and considering the result of their conduct, imitate their faith."

As we see above, when Jesus told us something was important, he also demonstrated that same trait in his own life. He taught the disciples to pray, and he also went off alone to pray. He told the disciples to serve others, and he washed their feet as an example. His words and actions matched up. Because of that, He was and is worth imitating. When we consider our lives before our children, here are some questions to reflect on.

FOR REFLECTION

- Do I want my children to imitate my life?

- What trait am I struggling to model well in my life? Or my marriage?

- How can I better model this in my life?

- What is one activity we can incorporate that would teach my child about this trait? (For example, if I dropped a jar of spaghetti sauce, I would intentionally tell my kids that I am frustrated but that it's not worth getting angry over. This would demonstrate self-control.)

6

Instilling Faith in Your Son

When I think of my sons' futures, many dreams come to mind. I hope and pray that they have happy marriages, successful careers, and meaningful lives with strong purpose using the unique gifts they have been given. (Okay, and I hope that they call me every day.)

Above all, I pray they leave my house with a personal relationship with Jesus. I truly believe that a relationship with Jesus—more than money, success, or even familial support—is the one thing that will prepare and sustain them through the inevitable ups and downs of life.

In fact, I often end heart-felt talks with my boys by saying, "But if you don't remember any other piece of advice that I've ever given you, then remember this: Falling in love with Jesus will be the best thing you can ever do for yourself."

And I mean it. Period. End of story. My sons having their own faith in Jesus is my ultimate dream; much like 3 John 1:4 says: "I have no greater joy than to hear that my children are walking in the truth." Yet I often wonder, like many other parents, "Are there habits that make a bigger impact in instilling faith in our children than others?" A study by Lifeway Research in 2016 found that answer to be yes.

In that study, researchers analyzed 2,000 Protestant and nondenominational adults who attend services at least once a month and have adult children ages 18 to 30 with strong faiths. The study found that certain habits, like having your child engage in prayer regularly, attend and serve in a church, listen to Christian music, and participate in mission trips or projects, helped children grow more spiritually.

But the biggest predictor of all was having your child read the Bible regularly as they grow up; this study found that children who did had a 12.5% higher spiritual health than their peers who did not. Simply said, instilling a strong faith in God happens when kids learn for themselves through Scripture who and what their faith is built on.

However, it's important to know that every family will choose to incorporate faith into their home differently. The research does emphasize some practices as more valuable than others, but it's important to give yourself grace in incorporating practices that build your son's faith into your home. God is bigger than following a cookie-cutter recipe.

For example, I love reading my Bible, but I didn't do scheduled weekly Bible studies with my parents or Scripture memory with my family growing up. Instead, I fell in love with it by watching my mom and dad read and discuss it with me, and by attending Bible studies with my youth group. I share this as comfort to remember there can be many means to the same end, so as you seek to instill faith, take time to pray and ask for wisdom and discernment from God for how to best lead your sons in habits that foster faith.

Practical Pointers

In chapter 2, we discussed which faith-based habits your son will likely be developmentally ready for from the toddler to teen years. But in this section, as you pray and consider what faith habits will be most meaningful in your home, I want to offer you some tips for instilling faith in your son.

DO!

Implement faith-building habits in your home that are meaningful to you and your son(s).

As mentioned previously, there are proven habits, like prayer, serving at church, and listening to Christian music, that are shown to help children develop strong faiths. But it's also important to incorporate habits that help you grow in your faith, as well as habits that mean something to your son. For example, I love Christian music (Christian rap, to be exact), so when I play it, I can't help but talk about its lyrics and meaning with my sons. It's a natural way to incorporate faith into our lives.

Prioritize Scripture.

Reading Scripture is shown to be the biggest predictor in help-ing kids stay spiritually healthy after leaving home. Incorporating Scripture into your home can involve a variety of habits, including having weekly Bible time, a nightly Scripture reading or devotional, Scripture memory at dinner, or something else God lays on your heart. There is no right or wrong way to learn Scripture. Instead, focus on what makes most sense for your family.

DO!

Keep faith personal to your son's life.

It is hard to feel compelled by faith if you don't understand its power in your life. Faith is meant to be practical, not abstract, so your son needs to not only hear Scripture, but also understand how its application helps his life. For example, when he is strug-gling with a friend upset with him, point out how, unlike humans,

God forgives every time He is asked. Simple connections like this make faith make sense and grow.

DON'T!

Get caught in rules or religion over relationship.

One of the most ineffective things we can do as parents is to make faith legalistic and rule-driven in our homes. Although we want to set habits in place to help our children grow, we also want to show grace to ourselves and our children in implementing those habits. If everyone has the stomach flu, then family devotion can wait until everyone is well.

DON'T!

Make your faith habits overwhelming or unattainable.

Sometimes our best efforts to incorporate faith habits into our home end up being overwhelming. Some families are successful with high structure and routine, but others struggle to have the same routine every day or week. For example, if sitting down and studying the Bible together as a family isn't happening, then free yourself to get creative and have family devotion in the car on the way to soccer.

DON'T!

Get caught in fear.

When you love something, you want others to love it, too, and it can be scary or upsetting if your children resist these things. If you notice a son being reluctant in receiving faith, be careful not to respond to this resistance with fear, because fear often causes unhealthy responses. Although we want our children to know the Lord, we have to remember that it is ultimately God that stirs their hearts toward Him. It is just our job to lead them to Him.

(Therapy tip: If you notice yourself being caught in fear over your son's lack of salvation, take time to pray and mentally hand his heart back to God, just like Abraham was willing to do with Isaac.)

What's the Word?

When I think of young people in the Bible with strong faith, I think of Timothy, who was converted to Christianity as a young man and worked closely with Paul, who wrote New Testament letters to him.

In 2 Timothy 1:5 (ESV), Paul tells us that Timothy's faith was passed down from his family: "I am reminded of your sincere faith, a faith that dwelt first in your grandmother Lois and your mother Eunice and now, I am sure, dwells in you as well."

Then, a few chapters later, Paul gives us more insight into the development of Timothy's faith in 2 Timothy 3:15 (ESV): "And how from childhood you have been acquainted with the sacred writings, which are able to make you wise for salvation through faith in Christ Jesus."

These Scriptures teach us that Timothy's mother had a strong faith that was passed to her son through the teaching of Scripture. It's a wonderful reminder to live out our own faiths and to keep our children within the Word of God. We also see another powerful example of instilling faith occurring between Paul and Timothy, where Paul is very intentionally taking time to teach and encourage Timothy to live out his faith.

He specifically instructs him with these words: "Don't let anyone look down on you because you are young, but set an example for the believers in speech, in conduct, in love, in faith and in purity. Until I come, devote yourself to the public reading of Scripture, to preaching and to teaching. Do not neglect your gift, which was given you through prophecy when the body of elders laid their hands on you." (1 Timothy 4:12–14)

If Paul knew that Timothy, who was already Godly, would benefit from specific instructions for Godly living, we should be intentional about teaching our children habits of faithfulness, too.

KEEP IN MIND

As you seek to bring habits of faith into your home, here are a few valuable reminders to keep your mind at peace when guiding the heart of your child.

Accepting Jesus is simple and possible for any child who is ready.

When your son comes to you and says he wants to accept Jesus, he may ask you what he needs to do. The Scripture below keeps this process very simple by telling us that we are saved by confessing that Jesus is Lord over our sin and that he died for us so that we could have eternal life.

"If you confess with your mouth that Jesus is Lord and believe in your heart that God raised him from the dead, you will be saved. For it is by believing in your heart that you are made right with God, and it is by openly declaring your faith that you are saved." (Romans 10:9–10 [NLT])

God is the only one that can save and ultimately change the hearts of our children.

"What do you think? If a man owns a hundred sheep, and one of them wanders away, will he not leave the ninety-nine on the hills and go to look for the one that wandered off? And if he finds it, truly I tell you, he is happier about that one sheep than about the ninety-nine that did not wander off. In the same way your Father in heaven is not willing that any of these little ones should perish." (Matthew 18:12–14)

God desires to offer us a life of freedom, not rigidity, through his Word and Spirit living in us.

"It was for freedom that Christ set us free; therefore keep standing firm and do not be subject again to a yoke of slavery." (Galatians 5:1 [NASB])

As we close this chapter, I encourage you to have a family meeting and choose faith habits to bring into your home. Talk with your spouse and son, and reflect on the questions below.

- What faith habit made the biggest impact on me when I was a child?

- What faith habit makes the biggest impact on me now?

- What faith habits do I see my child responding to with passion or excitement in our home?

- How can I incorporate these same habits into our home in a practical and not overwhelming way?

7

Setting and Respecting Boundaries

Boundaries. Some people love them. Some people hate them. Regardless of where you fall, healthy relationships need them, and loving parents, including our Heavenly Father, know we have to set boundaries for our children until they are old enough to do it for themselves. But parents also know that effectively getting our children to respect and value the boundaries we set can be easier said than done—especially if we have a child with a naturally rebellious spirit.

When I was in high school, I was on a trip with a friend and her little cousin. She was the cutest little thing, but everyone told me she was feisty, too. I got to see that feisty spirit firsthand when her mom told her that she could keep playing outside with me as long as she didn't cross a certain line near the lake we were visiting.

As her mom began to walk away, the little girl promptly walked right up to her mom, looked her square in the eye, touched her toe over the line her mom had just set, and then ran back toward me with a smile. It was clearly a rebellious move to her mom that said, "I won't fully cross your boundary, but I will get as close to it as I can." (Little did I know that moment was just a foreshadowing of what was to come with some of my sons in their toddler years.)

When we look to the Bible to see if boundaries are important to God, we quickly see boundaries are woven throughout Scripture, starting on the first pages of the Bible. Genesis 2:2 tells us that God set a boundary for himself by taking time to rest on the seventh day. We see Jesus setting a similar example in the New Testament when he retreats from crowds to go and pray.

We also see God giving his children boundaries of love and protection by giving Adam and Eve the boundary to not eat from the tree of good and evil. He also gives the Israelites the boundaries of the Ten Commandments.

Boundaries are important to God because they are His way of protecting us and our way of honoring Him. Boundaries are important between our children and us because they foster healthy relationships built on love, safety, and respect.

Parents who think love excludes boundaries must understand that Godly parents set reasonable boundaries that protect but also respect a child's autonomy until they are ready to protect themselves. This type of parenting style, discovered by prominent clinical and developmental psychologist Diana Baumrin, is called authoritative parenting. It should be the goal of all Christian parents because it is the same style in which God parents us.

Practical Pointers

Often when a parent-child relationship is struggling, it is easy to identify a boundary that is either misplaced or nonexistent. We are better parents with happier children when we create healthy boundaries. So, let's take a look at some guiding thoughts for helping us do just that.

Boundaries are necessary in Godly parenting.

If we want to parent our sons like God parents us, then we have to give our children boundaries. When I was little, I lived off a busy street, but I loved to play outside. One day before leaving for work, my mom took a can of gold spray paint and sprayed a line on the sidewalk, then told us, "When you play outside, don't go over the gold line." Maybe it was because it had shimmer or maybe it was because we could see the cars for ourselves, but my friends and I felt the love in the line and knew it was a boundary we didn't want to cross.

Boundaries involve physical, mental, emotional, and spiritual protection.

As parents, we need to feel empowered to not only protect our children from physical harm, but to also protect them from people or experiences that can hurt them mentally, emotionally, or spiritually. This might mean limiting the contact they have with a friend or stopping them from watching something that is contradicting their spiritual beliefs. Because our children are not old enough to do these things for themselves, it is our job to do our best to protect them.

Boundaries can change based on unique children and circumstances.

My friends and I took a group of young boys bowling for the first time this summer. At the start of the round, my friend and I asked them if they wanted the bumpers up to protect the ball from the gutter. They laughed at us and told us they didn't need any help. But after a few rounds where no one could keep their ball in the lane, they asked for the bumper. As parents, we should know boundaries can vary based on circumstance and need.

Parents should respect a child's request for reasonable boundaries.

If you've raised a son old enough to write sentences, then perhaps you've seen a note on his door that reads, "Keep out." This may be funny to see, but it is also a developmental step in independence when a child is asking for their boundary to be respected.

Even though we have ultimate say in the parent/child relationship, a healthy parent respects and listens to the boundaries their child requests, and allows them if they do not cause harm to the child or parent. For example, if they ask you to stop tickling them, it's important that you respect that boundary.

Boundaries can often be effective with understanding.

It's easy to assume your child will understand why you have put a boundary in place, but often they do not. I have some sons with a deep desire for control, so one of my most effective parenting methods is to explain why I put a rule in place. When they were little, I would calmly say things like, "Don't climb up the stair banister because if you fall, you can easily break an arm, and we will have to go to the emergency room." And it worked.

Parents need to demonstrate boundaries in their own lives.

Just as living out our faith is important, modeling boundaries to our children is also important. If we want them to respect our boundaries, then it's important to show that we respect others' boundaries, too. For example, if we expect them to have limits with screen time, we need to show that we limit our screen time, too.

What's the Word

Jesus was remarkable at showing us the value of setting boundaries, as well as the flexibility to step outside a boundary when it wasn't necessary.

Jesus was there for the people, but He knew when it was time to step away and be alone with God. "Yet the news about him spread all the more, so that crowds of people came to hear him and to be healed of their sicknesses. But Jesus often withdrew to lonely places and prayed." (Luke 5:15–16)

In Matthew 5:37, we also see that Jesus said to people that it's okay to say no—"All you need to say is simply 'Yes' or 'No'; anything beyond this comes from the evil one." He demonstrated the ability to say no when Herod asked Jesus to show some sign or wonder. Jesus knew his gifts were not for show, but for God's purpose, and He didn't budge.

However, we also see that those boundaries did not stop Him from doing God's work. When the Pharisees tried to accuse Jesus of working for food on the Sabbath, he responded to their trap by saying, "The Sabbath was made for man, not man for the Sabbath."

Jesus knew and believed that boundaries are made to help people, not to hurt them. And we need to remember this same powerful mindset when parenting our children.

As we conclude this chapter on the importance of boundaries, I want to empower you to look for areas where boundaries could strengthen the overall health of your home. Let's also use these final scriptures to reflect on a few additional concepts.

Fathers, do not exasperate your children; instead, bring them up in the training and instruction of the Lord.
Ephesians 6:4

It is also important as parents that we do not set boundaries that are unnecessary, because those types of boundaries frustrate our children and are often rooted in control or fear versus trust or love. When a child begins to feel trapped or controlled, they often begin to rebel. So, if your child is exasperated by your rules, take time to listen to their heart and respond.

"Do not be deceived: God cannot be mocked. A man reaps what he sows. Whoever sows to please their flesh, from the flesh will reap destruction; whoever sows to please the Spirit, from the Spirit will reap eternal life. Let us not become weary in doing good, for at the proper time we will reap a harvest if we do not give up." (Galatians 6:7–9)

God gives us boundaries in our faith for a reason. When we disregard those boundaries, we often reap pain. When Adam and Eve were deceived by the serpent and chose to eat from the tree of good and evil, they instantly became aware of their nakedness and felt shame, which serves as a powerful reminder to us and our children that God desires for us to respect his boundaries.

- Do I understand that boundaries represent love, not control? Are my boundaries rooted in something other than love?

- Do I have boundaries in place that love and protect my child both mentally, spiritually, and physically?

- Are there firmer boundaries that need to be set?

- Do I have unnecessary boundaries that should be removed?

8

Teaching the Value of Authority and Discipline

When I was in middle school, my dad and I were backing down my driveway on the way to my friend's house, and as we were pulling into the street, I asked him, "Do you care if I go ahead and stay the night with her, too?"

My dad answered by saying, "I need to talk with your mother first." I responded, "Can't you just make a decision for yourself without asking her?" He emphatically answered, "Why, yes I can. You aren't going anywhere tonight." And from that moment on, I knew that testing my dad in his authority was not something I wanted to do.

Christian parenting involves our sons understanding the value of authority in their lives and the need for discipline when they show a lack of respect toward that authority. Even though our children are being raised in a world where many feel they can treat authority any way they desire, Godly sons must learn that chaos ensues when people are raised with no respect for authority.

The book of Judges has a convicting phrase on this very subject that is repeated seven times, describing the days when Israel rebelled against God and ignored the warning of the leaders he sent to them. Judges 21:25 (NIRV) says, "In those days Israel didn't have a king. The people did anything they thought was right." We quickly see that their world crumbles every time they choose to disobey God and rebel against His protection.

Jesus knew this, and He made it clear to his disciples that He had authority over them and knew where that authority came from in Matthew 28:18: "All authority in heaven and on earth has been given to me." But, when we go back to the Ten Commandments in Exodus 20, we see that God set up a hierarchy for honoring authority, first by stating that we shall have no other Gods before Him, then by telling us to honor our father—even promising us a long life for obedience to this in Deuteronomy 5:16.

As we continue in the New Testament, we see that God also desires for us to submit to our earthly authority, saying in Romans 13:1, "Let everyone be subject to the governing authorities, for there is no authority except that which God has established. The authorities that exist have been established by God."

The Bible is also very clear that when we do not understand or respect God's authority, we are disciplined, not in anger or malice, but in a desire to train and correct us to become who God desires us to be. Deuteronomy 5:29 says it well: "Oh that their hearts would be inclined to fear me and keep all my commands always, so that it might go well with them and their children forever!" So, as we seek to raise sons who love the Lord, we must take time to discipline them for behaviors that rebel against authority, hurt others, or hurt themselves.

Practical Pointers for Godly Discipline

In keeping with the way God parents us, Godly parenting needs to show love, grace, mercy, and forgiveness toward our children, and it should also teach respect for our authority by using discipline to correct disobedience in our children. Here are some commonly asked questions in regard to this subject.

How do I increase obedience in my son?

Teaching your children about Biblical characters who obeyed God's authority (Noah, Abraham, Mary) versus those that didn't (Jonah, Saul, Judas), as well as pointing out real-life examples of people who have experienced significant consequences by disregarding authority, is a powerful teaching tool. Additionally, pointing out the effects of disobedience and disrespect for authority when it's in front of your children is helpful, too. It's important for a child to know that delayed obedience is still disobedience, so commending first-time listening is a great way to encourage it.

Parenting Tip: When you see your son is struggling with obedience, have him practice being obedient to you in small things. This may seem trivial, but it is a great way to remind your child what obedience should to look like.

Example: "Son, we are going to practice obedience right now. I want you to touch your head. Now your nose. Now your toys. Now pick up one toy." (For an older kid, "Now go put your clothes away.")

What role does respect play in authority and discipline?

Respect is a foundational principle within Godly relationships. For instance, it is never appropriate to use discipline as a way to shame or embarrass our children or to talk to them in a condescending tone. I encourage parents to avoid yelling as their go-to method of communication and reserve it for times when they need their child's immediate attention. Likewise, it should be expected that your child also shows you respect with actions and words. As parents, it is crucial we do not let small times of disrespect slide without correction. If they have a disrespectful tone, have them repeat their words respectfully so no habit of disrespect is built.

Parenting Tip: Discipline your child in a way that corrects them but also shows them respect.

Example: Find a word or signal for disrespect that alerts your child that they need to begin obeying immediately or they will receive discipline. In our family, I say my son's name and touch my nose. They know that if they don't straighten up quickly, a stricter form of discipline will follow.

Does the Bible promote spanking?

Spanking is a controversial disciplinary method for many, but some Christian parents wonder why the Bible has several passages mentioning the use of a rod—in reference to a shepherd's tool—for disciplining a child. When thinking of these passages in light of a shepherd using their rod and their staff to tend to their sheep, it paints a different visual of what discipline is about, considering Jesus calls himself the Good Shepherd and us His sheep. Discipline should never abuse or harm a child. Instead, it should change a heart.

What's the Word?

One of the most poignant and powerful parenting passages of Scripture that I've ever read regarding the value of obedience and authority is one (not surprisingly) that involves Jesus.

In the second chapter of Luke, Jesus and his family went to Jerusalem to celebrate the yearly Festival of the Passover. His parents left town, assuming Jesus was with them, but Jesus stayed behind in the temple asking questions and listening to people. The Bible says that those who heard him were amazed at his answers and wisdom, yet when his parents found him, they were understandably frustrated at his behavior and astonished by him.

Then, in Luke 2:48, we read this exchange between Mary and Jesus: "'Son, why have you treated us like this? Your father and I have been anxiously searching for you.'"

Lines 49–50 continue: "'Why were you searching for me?' he asked. 'Didn't you know I had to be in my Father's house?' But they did not understand what he was saying to them."

The passage ends by saying, "Then he went down to Nazareth with them and was obedient to them. But his mother treasured all these things in her heart. And Jesus grew in wisdom and stature, and in favor with God and man."

I love this powerful example of obedience. We see that at age 12 the boy, who would one day turn water into wine and bring the dead back to life, knew that He needed to go home and submit himself to the earthly authority of his parents to stay aligned with God's will.

This powerful example of God Himself choosing to submit to His parents is one to teach our children about, as well as to remind ourselves of, because if obedience was good enough for Jesus, then it should be a goal for us all.

Authority and discipline are two words that can make some people wince if they have been connected with harshness, anger, or pain instead of love.

If you are someone who struggles with these words because of your past, or if you are someone who is tempted to use discipline harshly, I want to close by redefining discipline as a way of redirecting our hearts back to respect of God, our parents, and others for the protection of ourselves and those around us. Here are a few final reminders as we close.

"All Scripture is God-breathed and is useful for teaching, rebuking, correcting and training in righteousness, so that the servant of God may be thoroughly equipped for every good work." (2 Timothy 3:16–17) Scripture is a great guide in knowing the best ways to correct, and for keeping out attitudes misaligned with God.

"Whoever loves discipline loves knowledge, but whoever hates correction is stupid." (Proverbs 12:1) Rebellion may make us feel powerful in the moment, but when we rebel against correction, we are actually showing foolishness. Because we learn and gain knowledge from the correction we receive.

"My son, keep your father's command and do not forsake your mother's teaching." (Proverbs 6:20) The Bible values obedience to authority and puts emphases on obeying our parents. It's important we teach our children the value of obedience and practice it within the home.

FOR REFLECTION

- Do my children respect my authority?

- Do I model respect for God's authority in my own life?

- Am I disciplining my children out of love?

- Are my discipline methods getting to the heart of my child?

PART THREE

Targeted Parenting Strategies

In this final section, my goal is to offer some specific strategies that will empower you to confidently address common parenting problems that you may encounter when raising boys. Every parent has to find what feels natural to them; these strategies are meant to serve as a resource for the various circumstances you may face.

9

Affirming His Sense of Identity and Self-Worth

W hen my third son was old enough to dress himself, he fell in love with baseball, so being Houstonians, we bought him a José Altuve shirt (a beloved player on the Houston Astros baseball team). From the moment he put that shirt on, we could barely get it off.

Whether he was sleeping or playing, he wanted that shirt on his body. It became a desperate matter when we had to wash it because he would stand at the washer and just cry as it went through the cycle. We even ordered another shirt that looked just like it, but he could tell the difference between the two and rejected the look-alike shirt.

Then, he woke up one day and told us he was done being a baseball player, and he picked up a police uniform from our costume shelf. From that moment on, he didn't just want to be a policeman, he was a policeman, and you couldn't tell him differently.

He wanted to get all the police gear, watch all the police shows, and visit all the police stations. We even had a police birthday party for him, where a whole squad of police came to our house with their lights flashing and sirens going for all his friends.

Then, after two years of wearing police uniforms, I walked by his room one day and noticed his police uniform had been hanging for a few days untouched. I asked him, "Why haven't you worn your uniform the last few days?" He answered, "Because I don't want to be a policeman anymore. I want to be an engineer like Daddy." And I remember my heart kind of broke because it was the end of an era. *Good-bye to my little policeman,* I thought to myself.

But then the next day, in true fashion to him, he walked into his closet and said, "Mommy, I want to start dressing like my brothers and wear sports clothes." And now, a few years later, he does just that. But his sports outfits always have to be black, and it doesn't matter if I buy him the coolest, most colorful shirt at the store. If it doesn't have black in it, it will just hang in his closet. So, black he wears.

But what can I say about this little guy other than he has always had a strong passion for expressing himself through his outward appearance. Although his identity has gone from a tiny baseball player in a dirty blue shirt to a shaggy-haired policeman with droopy pants falling off to a future engineer who loves wearing all-black sportswear—I know that my job is to forever point him back to his identity being rooted in Christ, as 1 Samuel 16:7 says, "People look at the outward appearance but I look at the heart." Because phases and interests will come and go in the lives of our children, but God's love for them will remain forever.

Practical Pointers

The world tells our sons that if they mess up, they will always be the sum of their past mistakes or struggles, but the Bible says in 1 Corinthians 5:17 that once they've accepted Christ (as discussed in chapter 6, page 62), they forever have a new identity of freedom and forgiveness in Christ: "Therefore, if anyone is in Christ, the new creation has come: The old has gone, the new is here!"

As Christian parents, we want to help our sons build such a strong identity in Christ that no matter what storms they face, if they look to His face, they will instantly be reminded of who they are through Him. And here's some simple ways to do that.

Teach your son that he is uniquely created by God and that gives him worth.

God created your son with careful intention and strong self-worth. If we want our children to feel confidence in who they are, they need to know that it was not themselves or even their mom and dad who chose their eyes, physical appearance, or even their personality traits. Instead, the Bible states it was God Himself who knit them together in their mother's womb. If we can help our sons truly grasp that the God of the universe created them with purpose before they even opened their eyes in this world, then their worth will be hard to diminish even in the hardest of times.

Teach your son that God doesn't play favorites, even if the world does.

God does not love one type of child more than another, nor does he have a preference for the type of child He uses for his purposes. But many people reject God because they see their own struggles and feel as if they are not good enough for God. It's important we teach and assure our children that despite any disability, difference, or struggle they might have, they will always be "good" enough for God to work in and through. His only prerequisite is acknowledgment of His death for their sins and acceptance of Him as the savior of their heart.

Teach your son that God is more concerned with his heart than his accomplishments.

This world tells us that our value comes from our activities and accomplishments: "You are a basketball player. You are an artist. You are a swimmer. You are an A student." But the Bible teaches that God looks at the heart and what comes out of it. Although extracurricular activities help build self-esteem and provide a fun outlet for children, they don't define their worth. Whether our children win or lose, are the smartest in the class or failing, their worth to God will never be in what they do, but rather in who God says they are—His children.

Teach your sons to follow God's plans and not anyone else's (including yours).

As parents, it can be easy to want our sons to fit into a certain mold. If we were athletic, we might want them to be athletic. If we were on student council, we might want them to also lead. If we were very social, we might not want them home on a weekend. But our plans for them are trumped by God's plans for them and who He desires them to be. The Bible tells us that God has plans for us (Jeremiah 29:11), and as Christian parents, we have to guide, protect, and lead our sons to the plan God has for them. Because strong self-worth in our sons is bred by pointing to a higher purpose in their life than any human desires.

FOR REFLECTION

Here are some questions to use for reflection to encourage and challenge you in raising sons with strong self-worth and strong identities in Christ.

- Does my son know his value comes from God?

- Does he know God will never love him more or less? Do I make sure my words match this truth?

- Am I placing too much emphasis on his accomplishments and not his character?

- Am I open to letting my son be someone different from who I am? (For instance, am I pushing him to be an athlete when he's an artist, or am I pushing him to be a musician when he prefers martial arts instead?)

- Am I placing my son in activities that support his unique gifts?

- Am I shaming my son for being someone different from what I desire, when instead I should be affirming who God has created him to be?

10

Cultivating His Passions and Interests

There's an old movie called *Field of Dreams*, in which a young Iowa farmer played by Kevin Costner feels led to build a baseball field in the middle of his cornfields at the urging of a mysterious voice that says, "If you build it, they will come." After he builds the field, the ghosts of great players start emerging from the crops to play baseball—including his father.

I often think about this line in regard to breeding passion and interest in the lives of our sons. I am a huge believer in parents inviting and encouraging creativity, imagination, and passion for life among our children (despite those passions often causing messes). We never know what might happen as a result when we foster a passion within them. A little boy who loves exploding soda cans may one day become a scientist. Or, a little guy who loves to make inventions out of your recycling may one day become an inventor himself.

I have one son who loves nature more than anything. From the time he was tiny, he loved animals, bugs, dirt, digging, and climbing—to the point that I often called him Tarzan. During our time in Covid quarantine, he became very interested in trying to build forts outside and kept asking how he could do it. So, instead of discouraging him, I bought him some scrap wood and rubber fasteners from the hardware store. Then, he and another boy began building forts in a grove of woods across from our house, and they were actually quite impressive. Soon, other children started to join them.

Because I could see they loved that spot so much, I bought a shovel for digging, a tree swing, and an obstacle course to put in the woods, too. Not long after, all the children in the neighborhood began showing up in this patch of trees to dig, build, and play in nature. And all I could think about every time I saw a pile of bikes parked across from my house was, "If you build it, they will come."

I think the same goes for building passion and interest in our children. Sometimes as parents, we get too comfortable saying no to our children when our children need us to say yes in order to help expose them to experiences that may reveal their talents and gifts. If we say no every time they show interest in something that is inconvenient or uninteresting to us, we may be preventing them from discovering something special inside of them. We may be raising the next Mozart or Steve Jobs or President of the United States, but we will never know unless we give them a chance to explore their gifts.

Practical Pointers

One of the most rewarding parts of parenting is seeing our children find what they care about and what they are gifted in. Some children may seem talented at everything, and others may seem to struggle more, but as parents, let's believe that within every child there is a gift to be discovered that can bring joy to themselves or others.

DO!

Expose your children to a variety of activities.

I think most parents have a certain standard of activities that we think to expose our children to, and sports is often at the top of that list, especially if we have sons. If our son isn't interested in sports, we are befuddled and might even feel he isn't passionate about much, but we must remember that there are *so* many more activities than just sports. Music. Acting. Dance. Martial arts. Art. Boy Scouts. Youth activities. Writing. Carpentry. Robotics. The list goes on and on.

DO!

Pay attention to what they are uniquely drawn to.

Each child of yours will likely have unique interests that may be similar to or different from their siblings' or peers'. Instead of assuming they will like the same things as those around them, pay attention to what things spur interest within them. Our older sons never touched markers, and our youngest son will draw detailed art for hours at a time.

DO!

Show passion for their interests.

My second son thrives on discovering new hobbies and is always finding something to be excited about, in addition to his ongoing passion for swimming. He's gone through phases of book writing, creating flip-books, building circuits, writing jokes, studying history, learning to skateboard, etc. Although I often see these phases come and go, I try to always join him in these hobbies because I understand that they are helping him discover who he is. Right now, he is immersing himself in learning how to skateboard, and I'm here to support it because I know God has created him to be someone with passion in this world.

DON'T!
Overlook what makes them different from others.

Ask yourself, "Is there a certain interest they have that makes them stand out?" We often don't notice the talents of our children because many of us assume all children are the same. But there may be talents or abilities in your children that others point out to you. Create ways to help those talents grow. You might have a child with an ability to draw beyond their peers, but you don't realize it until someone points out their gift. Or, you may have a child with a beautiful voice that you have overlooked because they have always sung since they were little.

DON'T!
Say no to things that you aren't interested in.

It's so tempting to discourage our children from being involved in activities that we don't care for and guide them toward the things we love. As parents, we do have the final say in what they are able to try, but make sure that you aren't saying no to something just because you don't like it—for example, if your son is begging you to join Boy Scouts, but you hate camping. Our interests should not limit theirs.

As you seek to help expose your son to things in which he may have unique passion and gifts, here are some questions to use for reflection.

- Do I believe my son could have a talent inside him that God desires to use for His glory?

- Am I noticing what my son is interested in?

- Once I notice, do I take time for those interests and ask questions?

- Are there more activities we could take part in to help him grow?

- What things do I need to stop saying no to and start staying yes to?

- Is there a past activity my son was interested in that I dismissed and now need to return to?

- Am I praying for ways to help foster growth within him for his future calling?

- Are there talents I have that need to be utilized more?

11

Arming Him with Emotional Coping Skills

E very day before my boys leave the house, I say a few words of encouragement to them. "Be a leader. Show others Jesus. Enjoy your learning. Make good choices. Avoid the kids making bad choices. And be kind to the kids around you." I often find myself overly emphasizing the ones involving their interactions with others. I will linger on "Be kind" and sometimes add, "even when it's hard."

I always check in with each of them after school; more often than not, I am met with a boring "It was good." But recently one of my sons hopped in the car and shared that a friend he normally eats lunch with got up and moved. I could hear the hurt in his voice. "What do you mean he moved?" I asked. "I mean, he raised his hand after I sat down next to him and asked if he could sit next to another boy," he said. My heart sank. I hate it when kids hurt.

So in true therapist fashion I asked, "So how did that make you feel?" He just shrugged his shoulders and started to get out of the car. I then shared a similar experience I had when I was a kid. "Well I know one time my friend did that to me, and I really felt hurt." He immediately popped his head up and said, "Yeah. It did hurt my feelings. But you've had it happen, too?" I explained that I checked with my friend to see if she was mad at something I did. She told me she wasn't mad at me, and this made me realize I needed to focus on other friends who wouldn't treat me that way. I encouraged him to do the same.

Before my sons left for school the next day, I said my usual phrases and this time I added, "And if a friend doesn't want to play with you, focus on playing with someone else." When my son came home that day, sure enough, his friend did the same thing. But this time he decided to play with someone else like I suggested, and he told me his day had been great.

I know that my job as a mom isn't to create a perfect world for my sons (even though I want to), but rather to equip them with emotional tools to handle the imperfect situations life throws at them. Christian boys need to not only know how to handle themselves, but also be able to navigate their own emotional world with wisdom and self-awareness.

Practical Pointers

Psalm 147:3 (NLT) says, "[God] heals the brokenhearted and bandages their wounds." If God cares enough about our hearts to bandage our wounds, we want our sons to be aware of and attuned to their own emotions and the emotions of others. Here are my best steps for building emotional intelligence in your son.

STEP ONE:
Identify situations where your son is struggling or hurting.

When you see a child is struggling in a situation, identify it as an opportunity to talk about it with them. For example: "I see you are upset about this situation. Your feelings matter to me and I want to hear all about it. Would you mind sitting down so we can talk?" Then, ask them questions. Engage with their heart and listen to their feelings and experiences without adding your emotions or perspective to it. (Note: Displaying your protective or angry Mama or Papa Bear side may feel like an empathic trait but is often unhelpful in situations when our children are hurting.)

STEP TWO:
Help your son identify and name what specific emotions he is feeling.

We don't just want our child to know they are upset, we want them to be more specific with their words and understanding of their emotions. In his book, *Raising an Emotionally Intelligent Child*, John Gottman teaches about a parenting style called emotion coaching that involves talking through hard situations and labeling emotions. I encourage you to read the book and increase your emotional vocabulary within your home.

If your child says they are mad at their friend, look for words that might help them understand their feelings even more accurately by saying things like, "Do you think you feel overlooked or rejected?" Saying you are sad is not the same as saying you are embarrassed. Saying you are tired is not the same as saying you feel defeated. Practice building a specific emotional vocabulary within your son.

STEP THREE:
Have your son think about the situation from the other person's viewpoint.

After you figure out how they feel, do your best to have your son consider the other person's viewpoint, too. The Bible says to love our neighbor as ourselves and to clothe ourselves with compassion, but we can't do that if we don't really understand what someone else might be thinking or feeling. Taking time to teach your son empathy for another person's experience strengthens not only their emotional intelligence, but also their ability to show God's love to the other person.

Help your son come up with a solution to their problem.

Once you understand the situation and really understand what they feel, help them come up with a plan or a tool. Be creative and brainstorm things that might work well with your son's personality. Have him practice what he would say and even how he would physically respond if it's a very uncomfortable situation. We can't assume our children know how to act unless we teach them.

STEP FIVE:
Offer Scripture as a comfort to strengthen your son.

If possible, find a Scripture that is relevant to their situation and offers not just human comfort, but also God's comfort and encouragement, and then pray with them. There is something that is so comforting about having someone arm you with prayers before you go into a hard situation.

STEP SIX:
Check in again after the situation.

Remember to check back in with your son about emotional situations. It shows concern and builds trust and teaches him to be compassionate when others are hurting, too.

FOR REFLECTION

One of the greatest tools we can offer our sons is the gift of emotional awareness. They will likely thank us for this gift as they mature, and their future spouses, friends, and children will thank us, too, because no one enjoys being around someone who cannot handle their emotions. As you consider the value emotional awareness adds to your son's life, consider these questions for yourself:

* Do I understand my feelings?

* Am I able to identify my emotions and talk about them with my children?

* Do I ignore problems or do I face them?

* Do I discipline my children when they are acting out but forget to help them talk through what they are feeling?

* Am I offering my son tools to handle hard situations?

* Do I get too worked up when my son is hurting and prevent him from wanting to share his experience with me?

12

Creating Strong Family Bonds

When I was growing up, my family and I would drive to Tulsa, Oklahoma, every few months to go visit Grandma Freda. We would help her clean her apartment, weed her flower beds, do her laundry, and run errands for her.

Of course, we mixed family traditions into our weekend visits, including going to a local donut shop and taking long walks down the Arkansas River, which weaved in and out of the surrounding neighborhoods of old mansions. We would also visit an art museum where my Mom used to play when she was little and eat greasy burgers at on old diner.

When I look back on the memories of visiting my grandma, I remember cleaning, but I also remember loving it. I think it's because it was clear that we were joining together as a family to help but also enjoying our time together in the process. Sometimes when I'm feeling nostalgic about my childhood, I will even look up flights to Tulsa just to see how easily I could make it there and back. The first place I would want to visit is her old apartment, where I spent so many hours with my family.

I didn't know it then, but what my parents were doing was something the Mayan culture calls "acomedido," which is raising kids that are willing to help their parents. For a recent book called *Hunt, Gather, Parent,* Michaeleen Doucleff studied parenting strategies from Mayan families in Mexico, Inuit families above the Arctic Circle, and Hadzabe families in Tanzania. The author found that these cultures didn't have the same parenting challenges that Western parents did because they built relationships on cooperation, trust, and moment-to-moment needs. This created families with strong bonds.

The Mayan parenting style allows and encourages children and parents to join in on an activity instead of separating out activities for adults and children. This type of parenting requires a willingness to be patient with children as they learn to do things, but it also creates helpful children who are connected and willing to help their families because their lives are centered on what "we" do together versus what "I" am going to do.

When I consider the research around this parenting style, I can't help but note that strong bonds are created within families when we teach our children to see themselves as a valuable member of a collective family unit, versus an individual person who lives with a family but does what they want. Our culture often applauds independence, but the Bible teaches us we are more powerful when we support each other with love, as Colossians 3:14 (ESV) reads: "And above all these put on love, which binds everything together in perfect harmony."

Practical Pointers

Creating strong family bonds today is what keeps families strong and connected in the years to come. Here are some practical do's and don'ts to create healthy relationships of trust and support now that will foster connection with your children as they grow.

DO!

Look for everyday ways to create rituals of connection within your home.

Sometimes parents forget that we can connect and make strong bonds with our children through everyday activities. The ritual you do at bedtime. The game you play on Saturday nights. The waffles you make on Sunday mornings. All of these are building family bonds.

Forget to break away from daily habits to create special memories, too.

Sometimes we do need a break (especially as adults) from the daily routine to relax, decompress, and have time away from distractions. Vacations, concerts, or special events are simple ways to step away from the everyday world and connect with your family. Creating special memories does not have to involve a large budget—driving the family to a park for the day or doing a nature walk provides the same intent to connect.

DO!

Create a family mission statement.

Businesses, schools, churches, and various organizations have mission statements with a collective list of values and goals written out to remind its members who they are. This same concept can have great value within a family by creating bonds and unity between its members—especially when sitting down to write it. When I first had boys, I wrote a mission statement for the type of boys I wanted to raise in my home and posted it on my refrigerator. It served as a reminder to me and my sons of what mattered most in our home.

DON'T!

Exclude your children from everyday tasks.

Instead of separating everything into "my" adult tasks and "your" kid tasks, let your child join you in your world. When your child asks to help you fold laundry, cook chili, or clean the car, it's easy to want to say no, because let's be real, kids can often make a big mess when trying to join us. But saying yes is actually an opportunity to bond, build your child's sense of ownership in the family, and teach them to be helpful and productive.

DON'T!
Buy into the myth that siblings hate each other.

Our culture often supports the notion that siblings can and will drive each other crazy, but I disagree and believe parents can help break this belief through their parenting. Parents can build the sibling relationship by pointing out the sweet things their children can do for each other, asking them to speak respectfully of one another, and reminding them often of the lifelong friend God has given through a sibling.

DO!
Have individual dates with your children.

Whether you have a big family or a small one, taking time to have individual dates with your child is important. One family I know takes time to connect with their child each month on the day of their birthday (Example: If a child has a birthday on 9/17/13, then they take that son out on the 17th of the month.) You don't have to do a big date. It can be simple times together like getting groceries and going for ice cream after.

FOR REFLECTION

Strong family bonds are created and strengthened through love, time together, and creating shared meaning in family activities. As you consider the value of strong family bonds and connections, here are some questions to consider.

- Have I created family traditions with my children? If not, what are some traditions I can begin to create?

- Have I created a family mission statement? Is there a team name I could give my family to be called upon when unity is needed?

- Do I welcome the presence of my children in my everyday activities, or do I segment them off in a separate child world? If I do separate, what are some simple activities I can welcome them into where they can learn and feel like a part of the family?

- Do I put too much emphasis on needing big experiences to create bonding, versus finding ways to connect in small moments?

13

Managing Conflict in the Family

I have a son who was born running early, and I mean that literally. He was born a week early, and ever since then he never wants to be late for anything. Being "on time" to him really means showing up 20—or even 30—minutes early.

He definitely did *not* get this running-early trait from his father or me. I'm the type of girl who is more than comfortable walking up to an event that begins at 6:30 right as the clock switches from 6:29 to 6:30 without a hint of anxiety in my bones. Ironically, I tend to get more anxious when I am early.

This difference in our personalities has caused quite the opportunity for conflict between us throughout the years. After all, our family of six has three other brothers who aren't in a hurry ever, even if my husband and I are doing everything we can to rush them and ourselves.

This conflict is ever present on Sunday mornings, when everyone is rushing to get ready for church. My son, who is usually ready an hour early, slowly goes from a gentle encourager to a firm-but-scary coach to a crazed drill sergeant, yelling at his brothers to brush their hair faster and find their shoes or else. We often leave the house with everyone bickering and pull up to the church in an emotional state. I laugh as I write this because I see the utter irony here.

One day, we tried a few new habits that showed mutual respect for everyone's wishes. For a few weeks, either my husband or I would leave *extra* early with the impatient son, and one of us would arrive on time with the other boys. After our experiment, we asked him if anything bad happened when we arrived on time to church. Our son smiled coyly and said, "You're right. I guess it isn't that bad when you show up on time."

The truth is, we didn't make the problem of arriving early go away, but we did succeed in demonstrating that we may not agree with his feelings, but we did care about his heart. That mentality is what Godly conflict management is all about.

Practical Pointers

The word *conflict* often has negative feelings attached to it, but conflict is an opportunity for connection if love and respect stay at the center of the communication. Teaching our children to handle conflict with others, not with extreme emotions but with reasonable responses, will strengthen their relationships.

Six Tips to Handle Conflict as a Parent

1. **Remember conflict is healthy.**
   Relationships with no conflict are not necessarily healthy because it often means someone is not expressing their wants or needs. It may be possible for two people in a relationship to agree on everything, but most people do not see eye-to-eye on every issue. It's fair to say God doesn't intend for us to all think alike. It's why He gave us free will. Therefore, disagreement will arise in healthy relationships built on honest and open communication.

2. **Listen empathetically first. Fix later.**
   When you don't know what else to do with a child you are disagreeing with, you can start by just listening. Listening with an empathetic and non-defensive heart can emotionally move mountains by giving your child a safe haven to say what they

need. As they share their heart (even if it's angry), repeat back to them what they are expressing, whether you agree or not. For example, "So you feel your Dad and I spend all our time criticizing you instead of noticing what you are doing well? And that hurts you?" There is power in accepting someone's emotions, and often when we do this, we see a softened heart as a result.

3. **Recognize that anger is the tip of the iceberg, and the real emotion is underneath.**
When you are dealing with someone who is angry and yelling, try to widen your lens and consider the bigger picture. We often see the anger at the surface, but it's just a signal that more is going on underwater. When we go below the surface, we can respond to the underlying emotion—not just anger—which is more helpful because matching anger with anger often shuts down communication instead of fixing the conflict.

4. **Healthy conflict does not mean all emotions or words should be expressed.**
Not saying anything during conflict is unproductive, but saying everything when you feel angry or emotional can be dangerous. It is important to address the feelings behind the anger by saying how you feel versus showing how you feel. For example: A mom calmly saying, "I am very angry you chose to lie to me. It hurts my feelings because I don't feel respected," will likely produce a more effective result than a mom yelling, "I am soooooooooo angry at you for being a liar! What a disappointment you are!" Refrain from expressing emotions that spew anger, bitterness, or rage.

5. **When our children have expressed themselves, demonstrate a desire to repair.**

My favorite thing to say to someone who is mad at me or hurting in front of me is, "How can I help you right now?" When a parent asks this, a child normally answers with "I need this . . ."—whether they are 5 years old or 15. We want our children to see that even in the midst of struggle, we are there for them. For younger children, getting down to their eye level is particularly helpful in calming them down.

Conflict is a part of all relationships, including parent and child, and teaching our children how to handle conflict is one of the greatest tools we can give them for success. As we close this chapter, consider teaching and discussing these three valuable lessons with your son.

You can and will disagree. And that's okay.
"I want you to know that we are not always going to see eye to eye on everything, because God created you individually just as he created me. We don't have to see everything the same to love each other."

Care about his feelings, but be respected.
"My goal when we are disagreeing is to hear your perspective and find a solution to our disagreement. However, during the process, I cannot be disrespected by you. You can disagree with me, but you cannot yell at me, call me names, etc. Or you will be disciplined for the disrespect."

The goal is to find peace, but God has given the parent authority over the child for protection, and that has to come first.
"Although I want to find solutions to things that make you and me happy, there are times where I will make decisions you don't agree with because I am your authority. And it's important you know that these decisions are made because I do love you and not for any other reason."

14

Handling Physical Changes and Hygiene

I've had my house full of little boys for the last decade, but I'll never forget the day a group of middle school boys walked in after playing a game of football in the street, and I had to step out of the room because of the smell of body odor. I pulled my son aside in our pantry as if I had something very serious to say and said, "Hey, one of your friends really needs deodorant. Go spray him with air freshener." He just laughed at me, and I started laughing, too.

As we walked back into the kitchen, I kept looking around to see if the other boys would notice the smell, but instead, they all just kept goofing off, probably because they all smelled bad! So I did what all moms who want smelly boys out of their house do and offered them popsicles outside. As soon as they left, I texted their moms and said, "I know what our boys need for Christmas," and sent them a picture of a bottle of Axe body spray.

This started a whole comical conversation about the changes we were all seeing in our sons, and it just made me smile. When our sons were little, we talked about the tooth they had coming in or about getting them to say enough words, but now we were talking about the hair growing on their faces and the strange cracks in their voices.

I'll never forget the day my son screamed my name at the top of his lungs from his room. I ran upstairs as fast as I could only to see him looking under his arm with a smile. "Look, mom.

I'm becoming a man." And as he showed me his first lone arm hair, I fought back tears. Once he saw my emotion, he couldn't help but bring me back down to planet earth. "It's okay, mom. I'm not leaving the house yet. It's just one hair." I just tightly hugged that baby boy of mine with his one lone arm hair because part of raising kids is watching them grow, just as God intended.

Practical Pointers

Puberty can be awkward or alarming for children, but one of the best things about puberty and the changes that happen as a result is that every child goes through these changes, which means every parent experiences them, too. Our role as parents is to be sensitive to the way our sons feel about these changes and arm them with both the physical and emotional tools to handle these changes with confidence. As you do this, here are some do's and don'ts to keep in mind.

Answer all his questions.

With puberty, when children ask us questions, we answer, and we normalize all the things they want to understand. "So why is my penis bigger than it used to be? Why is my penis smaller than such-and-such? Why do I have facial hair? Why do I smell like a gorilla? Why does my face have so many pimples?" Instead of giving short and uneducated answers, it's important we truly do our research if we don't know.

Act awkward about his changes.

You set the tone for everything in your house, including how your son feels about his changing body and his budding sexuality. God intentionally created childhood for a season, but it isn't meant to last forever, so it's important we normalize the growth process in our sons, even when they find it odd. Don't joke about their changes unless they feel comfortable with who they are, and remind them how much God intended and desired this process of maturity to occur.

Teach him proper hygiene and provide supplies.

Puberty can be hard for a child if they don't take care of themselves and other people notice, especially their peers. Therefore, it is important that our children know the value of showering regularly, wearing deodorant, properly caring for their skin, and learning how to shave if they have facial hair. We don't want to overly focus on their body and appearance to the point that it makes them self-conscious, but we want to aid them in managing these new parts of themselves by buying them things like deodorant, razors, and pimple cream and teaching them how to use these products.

Forget to respect his boundaries.

It's sometimes hard to believe that the little boy you bathed for years, and who broke into the bathroom every time you shut the door, now needs privacy from you. But he does. Once his body begins changing, it is important that you treat him as an adult and don't walk in unannounced while he's dressing or showering. You may or may not feel comfortable seeing his maturing body because he's your son, but he may not feel the same, so respecting his privacy is key.

DO!

Be sensitive to his feelings.

Puberty can produce a lot of feelings in your son that are sometimes predictable and sometimes not. For instance, as much as many boys prefer to be tall, your son might feel awkward if he grows faster than any other boy in his grade and hits six feet before his friends are five feet. So, be sensitive to the feelings of your son during this time, and assure him that God created his unique body just as He intended.

FOR REFLECTION

When your son hits the age of 9 and 10, ready or not, here puberty comes. Even if you don't feel ready to guide him through it, your job is to do just that. So here are some questions to ask yourself as you seek to be his teacher.

- Have I taught my son about puberty? Does he know what to expect?

- Does he understand God desires him to become mature?

- Am I comfortable talking about body parts? If not, what do I need to do to normalize this?

- Have I made it clear that I am here to answer anything?

- Do I answer his questions in detail, or do I just try to end the conversation?

- Have I equipped him with tools to groom himself?

- Am I teaching him coping skills to help him handle situations that may make him feel awkward? (For example, when others ask him, "Why are you so tall?" teach him to have a response that makes him comfortable. "Because some people have to be able to reach the top shelf.")

15
Dealing with Bullies

My son got in the van the other day after swim practice, exasperated, and emphatically said, "Brooks is a bully!" as he angrily slammed the door, and then added, "And I don't like swimming next to him." As he buckled his seat belt, I asked him what had happened, and he went on to tell me several stories about Brooks.

"Well, when the coach went to line us up today, he told us to line up according to our time, so I got in line and Brooks cut in front of me and said, 'Get out of my way! You're little!' But I told him, 'We are supposed to line up by times not size.' And he said, 'Well, I'm faster than you.' Then my two friends told him that I was faster, but he wouldn't listen. And wouldn't budge.

When I went into the swim lane, the coach put him next to me. We were supposed to leave every 30 seconds for the drill, but he kept leaving early and telling me he beat me. He was cheating, Mom, and just wouldn't listen. The other boys said he does it to them, too."

The day my son told me about Brooks, we spent the rest of our car ride home talking about reasons Brooks may act like this, ways my son can respond, and the things my son can remember in his heart and mind to not feel so frustrated. Our job as Christian parents is not to be surprised when our child is bullied, but instead to equip them with techniques to deal with the bullies they encounter in their lives.

No one likes a bully, but it seems most everyone has had to deal with them at one point or another in life. Since people have been around, bullies have been around, too, so it is important we arm our children with tools to deal with bullies and remind our boys that God will be with them, as Deuteronomy 31:6 teaches: "Be strong and courageous. Do not be afraid or terrified because of them, for the Lord your God goes with you; he will never leave you nor forsake you."

Practical Tips

When your child is dealing with a bully, it is important to equip him with tools and emotional support to work through it.

5 STEPS TO TEACH YOUR SON HOW TO HANDLE A BULLY

1. **Help your son identify what bullying is and isn't.**
   To protect against bullies, your son needs to know that bullying is not just a onetime joke. It's a frequent occurrence where someone uses their power or influence over your son with their words or actions to make him feel bad about himself or hurt him in some way.

2. **Identify if there is an easy way to stop the situation.**
   Pacifying this person (like choosing to help the bully in science class instead of the bully forcing your son to give him answers) and limiting interactions with this person (like moving to the front of the bus) are simple steps to stop a situation. Also, consider shutting down a social media account to prevent cyberbullying. Sometimes a simple interaction can stop a bad interaction from building.

3. **Teach your son to display confidence toward the bully in a non-emotional way.**
   Bullies tend to pick on kids they can trigger. It's not fun to fight with someone who isn't bothered by you, so teaching your son to stay calm (which can be challenging) is a powerful tool!

Here are three responses for your son to use when a bully tries to engage him.

- **Say "Stop."** Encourage your son to confidently tell the bully to stop. Something as simple as, "Dude, stop. That's not cool," can show the bully your son isn't going to put up with just anything.

- **Be quick, and roll with the insults.** Teach your son to be ready with a quick responses if a bully is trying to insult them. If a bully says, "Dude, you look like a leprechaun with that red hair," have your son say something like, "Yep, I got the luck of the Irish." When you joke with a bully, it can disarm them by taking away their control.

- **Act as if you don't notice their mean intent.** In general, the less response you show to a bully, the less rewarding that action will be. If they take your book bag and throw it, and you keep talking to your friends as if it didn't happen, it takes power from the bully and gives it back to the victim.

4. **Teach him to tell an adult if he is in harm's way.**
   If a bully is causing your child emotional stress or physical harm in any way beyond what they feel they can manage, teach them to tell an adult. In fact, I suggest encouraging your child to tell an adult the moment a bullying incident occurs, so they can stop it in its tracks when they see it.

5. **Talk to him about the power of staying near adults or groups of kids.**
   Lastly, kids can avoid being bullied when they avoid going places alone and stick close to their peers. If they want to let a situation de-escalate with a person or avoid something from occurring, teach them to wait for a friend or adult to walk the hall, leave school, or get on the bus.

Here are few final questions to reflect on when teaching our kids to stand up against bullies.

Does my child understand bullies are often suffering?
From a Biblical standpoint, it's important that our children know that bullies are often sad kids inside who show mad tendencies on the outside. Well-adjusted kids don't feel a need to put other people down. When a child understands this truth, they can sometimes build more confidence to stand up to their bully when they remember that child is hurting, too.

Does my child understand that bullies target not only those who are weak, but also those they admire?
Although we often assume it is the unpopular kids that get bullied, sometimes it's the ones who everyone likes. If your child thinks this person is bullying them because they are jealous, discuss ways your son might promote peace in the relationship.

Can I answer these questions?

- Is there a witty response I can teach my child in response to a bully?

- Are there simple tools I can teach my child to arm themselves with more confidence?

- In the case of cyberbullying, does my child need social media accounts? Can he go without them?

16

Broaching Love, Sex, and Relationships

I was born a bit boy crazy. Okay, a lot. From second grade on, I can't remember a time I didn't have a boyfriend in some way, shape, or form. I received my first gift from a boy in third grade. It was an impressively large bag of quarters that wooed my heart more than you can imagine. Now, I was finally able to go try the new Cookie Dough Blizzard at Dairy Queen.

In fifth grade I received a mystery Valentine's Day card from the boy in my carpool that said, "Do not open until you get home." I didn't know it was from him and opened it in his mom's car on the way. That's when I discovered it was a picture from him saying, "I love you." The ten minutes that followed were some of the most awkward in my life, but from that moment on, I followed directions on cards.

In sixth grade, my husband—who would assuredly tell you he knew we would marry from the first moment we met— actually proposed to me in our school yearbook. He wrote, "Will you marry me in 10 years?" And we did 10 years later.

My sister, on the other hand, never dated much until her late twenties, and ended up happily married just the same. When I reflect on our parents' guiding us through dating, I remember my mom giving me parameters to keep me out of trouble: "Dating is a place where we can learn a lot about what we do and do not want in a future spouse." Those words turned out to be very true.

Now that I have four sons with varying personalities, it's clear their experiences will be different, too. One, just like his Dad, has loved the same girl since he met her four years ago. Another gets notes from little girls right and left, but seems pretty aloof about it.

But the other night when my sons were asking me about dating, I found myself surprised at my own advice: "Dating isn't bad. But it presents a lot of challenges and keeps you focused on things that may not last but overlooks things that will, so there is no rush to date."

One of my boys quickly responded, "But didn't Dad propose to you in middle school?!" I had to smile.

The truth is, I don't regret dating, because it did teach me a lot about who I was and what I wanted, but it should be handled with care.

Practical Pointers

Dating is an opportunity for emotional growth, social learning, and fun. It can also bring stress, heartbreak, and distraction. Parents have to find what works for their family. Here are some tips to keep in mind as you help your son navigate dating.

Create reasonable guidelines that respect you, your son, and his relationships.
We often don't think about reasonable guidelines for dating until our child first shows interest in someone. Then, suddenly you're catapulted into deciding if you want them alone together, texting all day, or telling each other "I love you." Guiding lovestruck teens with empathy and flexibility in setting boundaries is often more helpful than drawing rigid lines.

A helpful mindset to teach your son is that dating is all about building a strong friendship and emotional connection, and friendship doesn't need to be sexual. (For example, you may not allow your son to be alone with someone he likes, romantically, in his room, but you may feel okay if you chaperone them to the movies.) Set boundaries to support building an emotional connection, but remember that God has given you authority and wisdom to look out for your child and say no when necessary.

Teach your son how to handle himself with integrity.
You may assume your son knows how to demonstrate strong character when in a romantic relationship. But in reality, he will likely not know what he's doing unless you teach him. Take time to talk to him about things like manners, etiquette, God-honoring words, and respect for his partner's physical boundaries. The more you teach, the more they grow in character.

Parenting Tip: In the digital age we live in, it is crucial your son understands that every picture and text he sends can be used against him for years to come. Repeatedly remind him that anything he sends via text or email needs to be something he's okay for a whole crowd to read or see.

Stay attuned to his heart. But keep yours out of it.
Ask your son how his relationship is going, and get to know his significant other. If he seems stressed about a situation, allow him to talk to you about it, then give guidance. If he's heartbroken, don't minimize his feelings or make light of the situation. Similarly, if he's done with a relationship, don't insert your feelings. You will be most effective in parenting when you look at his relationships as ways to connect with others, learn about himself, and love in the process.

Teach your children about sex and the consequences.
God created sex as a beautiful part of marriage, yet many Christian teenagers understandably struggle with the temptation to have it before that time. As we seek to guide our sons in sexual purity, it's helpful to teach them that God desires sex to be for marriage, and that is not because He wants to be mean or cruel. He knows that sex outside of wedlock often causes hurt, unhealthy emotional attachment, and sometimes more serious consequences like teen pregnancy and disease.

Love, sex, and relationships are some of the greatest gifts in life, as well as some of the most complicated. Because of this, we need to be prayerful, compassionate, wise, and diligent in the way we guide our sons.

- Have I taught my son about healthy relationships?

- Have I put safeguards in place to protect his heart?

- Am I checking in with my son about sexual temptation? Addiction?

- If my son is struggling with any issue, does he feel comfortable telling me?

Therapy Tip: There are hot topics in the Christian world related to love and sex that often produce controversy, including sexual addiction, homosexuality, and gender identity struggles.

Although these topics are more complex than this chapter can handle, I encourage you to remember that our ultimate goal as Christian parents is to point our sons to their own relationship with Jesus so Jesus can work in their lives and hearts as they grow. When our sons bring something to us that contradicts Scripture, we may feel inclined to dismiss their struggle altogether.

I want to remind you that we lose our influence to teach and guide them about right and wrong when we reject or shame our sons for a sin or struggle they have. Listen, talk, and pray with your sons, and encourage them to invest in their relationship with Jesus. No matter how you feel about any of these challenging topics, I encourage you to meet your sons with love when they bring their heart to you, just like Jesus meets you with love, and then point them back to Him.

17

Navigating the Internet, Social Media, and Video Games

M y boys were swimming in the backyard with their dad when my phone dinged with an alert from a friend: "Hey, I really need to talk with you. Blake just told me something after coming home from a trip with friends."

I called my friend, whose voice was noticeably shaken, and she instantly blurted out the news about her 11-year-old son. "Blake told his friend he's been looking at porn. And he felt like he needed to tell me, too."

With a tearful voice she said, "I just don't understand how this happened. We have filters on his devices, and he knows that it's not a good thing to do." She told me how heartbroken she felt at what he had seen and how desperate she felt to protect his mind and heart.

Then, just a week later, another friend texted me and said, "Hi, can you talk with my best friend? She just found out her eight-year-old has been looking at porn. And she's devastated. And so is he." As soon as I read it, I had to take a seat because I was standing next to my own eight-year-old son, who seemed so little and innocent. *Porn at age eight,* I reflected silently.

And my heart just broke.

When I called the family, I learned that the son's older friend found some enticing accounts on Instagram and TikTok that led him to getting curious and searching for more on the Internet. Once he found it, he was hooked and started showing his friends. He was just a child himself, so he didn't think twice about exposing an eight-year-old to inappropriate sexual content.

As you read these stories, you may be shocked to hear that young boys are struggling with pornography because it feels like such an adult issue. However, that is exactly what technology offers our children—it contains both helpful information that is appropriate for young eyes and destructive and harmful adult content that you would never want young eyes to see. The only boundaries that determine what content our sons are exposed to at a young age is the safeguards we put in place.

Technology can serve as a convenient babysitter to tired parents, especially when kids are happy and quiet. If we allow our children to have it, then we must have respect for its ability to be misused. Early childhood educator and *New York Times*–bestselling author Erika Christakis states it best: "More than screen-obsessed young children, we should be concerned about tuned-out parents."

When parents are intentional with teaching their children to respect technology, use it for good, and understand the reason why some things are off-limits, its presence can remain a positive and helpful tool for our children to have more knowledgeable, connected, and convenient lives. (And to have no excuse not to pick up the phone when we call.)

Practical Pointers

Raise your hand if you've ever told a child to get off technology and then realized you were holding your own phone. Most parents want their children to spend less time on technology, but the average American spends 6.4 hours per day on their phone, as reported by ZD Net.

This means that if we want our sons to have a healthy relationship with technology, then we must model a healthy relationship with technology within our homes. Here are two primary tenets to consider when teaching your son.

Technology has benefits but deserves respect.
Living in the 21st century has many perks. Technological advancements have made our day-to-day lives more convenient and efficient in areas like communication, healthcare, and business, but there may be adverse emotional and behavioral effects on our children's brains when they spend hours behind a screen or phone instead of playing outside or engaged in real-life activities. A Finnish study examining psychosocial effects of technology on preschool-age children found that children who exceeded the recommended limits of screen time demonstrated increased struggles with peers, hyperactivity, and conduct problems when compared to those who had less screen time. As parents, it's important to teach our children that in order to experience the benefits of technology, we also have to respect that too much of it can have negative effects.

Technology is respected by creating boundaries and safeguards.
Many things can be bad for us in excess, and many things can be good for us with boundaries. Since we cannot make technology go away for our children, our job is to set and model good limits of self-control. There are many websites that allow you to create a technology contract with your child. I encourage you to consider creating family contracts to set clear boundaries in regard to technology. But as you do this, here are additional guidelines to keep in mind.

VIDEO GAMES

- Do monitor what games they are playing, and be mindful of the level of violence.

- Do monitor how much time they spend playing, and set limits.

- Do make sure they are not connecting with strangers and sharing information about themselves.

- Do consider having them balance time gaming with time spent on other activities.

PHONES

- Do check their phone and texts regularly.

- Do consider using a protection content filter of some kind.

- Do ask them to charge their phone outside of their bedroom.

- Do have family times where phones aren't allowed. (Dinner and bedtime are easy times to do this.)

- Do set screen time limits and mute notifications.

- Do remind them that anything they send via text can be used against them and shown to others in a split second.

SOCIAL MEDIA

- Do consider if your child needs a social media account.

- Do research on the platform you agree to let them join.

- Do understand inappropriate and explicit content is a part of *all* social media platforms.

- Do set guidelines for language and visuals that are not allowed in their posts.

- Do teach them about dangers of friendships with strangers on social media.

FOR REFLECTION

It can be easy to let our children have their own online world and assume all is well. But, you may never know your child is sending mean texts, getting bullied, or looking at inappropriate content unless you check in. If you give your child a tool as powerful as a phone, then you need to monitor it, too.

Ask yourself: Do I monitor my child's phone daily?

Families, including parents, need time when no one is on technology. Technology can negatively affect us by distracting us from meaningful connections with our families, keeping us overly connected to work or raising our anxiety without us even knowing it, which can cause us to be stressed and rude.

Ask yourself: Does my phone keep me disengaged from my child? Are there times when I am mindful about putting it in another room?

As mentioned previously, technology can keep our children engaged and happy and make our lives easier as parents. However, children also need real-world interactions where they gain social skills that teach them how to work with others and connect in conversation.

Ask yourself: Am I making efforts to keep my child connected in the real world?

18

Diving In When Your Son Is Acting Out

When I was a senior in high school, I wrote a college scholarship essay that began with the words, "Flexibility yields happiness, or at least that is what I've come to believe at the ripe age of 18." The words of that essay went on to earn me a full scholarship to the journalism school at Kansas State University, and 20 years later, that line remains one of my greatest beliefs in life.

Because anger and anxiety are like viruses that spread when we willingly cough them out on each other, I do my best to quickly reset so I don't spread that negativity to others. When tempted to be rude, I do what I can to be flexible and kind instead, knowing that no one enjoys being angry or stressed.

So, you can imagine my surprise when I started having children and discovered that toddlers can be moody. Instead of being boys who wanted to be like their mama and move through negativity, their method was to try to drag me down into their misery (literally and metaphorically) and make me sit in it, like Jacob wrestling the angel in the Bible.

My idealistic, magical parenting method was to say, "Stop, this behavior is unacceptable." (Which I definitely thought would work before having children.) Their metaphorical response back to me was, "I accept your disdain. And I'll raise you one." I found myself tired and wanting to cry out, "Check, please." But I couldn't check out because they needed me.

One day, I was in the middle of working through a particularly hard phase in parenting when my cousin came to visit. Her young daughter had a complete meltdown deserving of an Emmy. Instead of acting agitated or bothered that it was going on, my cousin sat down with her in the middle of my kitchen floor, got on her eye level, and just held her as she kicked and screamed. My instinct was to open the front door so my cousin could run away for a moment, but she instead dove right into the struggle, just like Jesus does for us.

In parenting, there are days when we feel we are doing nothing right, but we are wise to know those times won't last forever when consistent love and patience are involved. About a year ago, I was in a challenging phase with my son and felt I was seeing no payoff from my best parenting efforts. And a year later, this same son is doing so well in life that I can't imagine feeling prouder of his character.

When my friend asked me what we had done to see such growth in him, I jokingly answered back, "Really nothing. Just a little talking. Teaching. Praying. Checking in. Talking more. Teaching more. Checking in more. Talking more again. And praying." If we want our sons to have Godly character, we don't run when they act out; instead, we dive in.

Practical Pointers

Don't compare your son or life to others.

When you have a child who is struggling, avoid comparing them or your life to any other child or parent. Comparison is the thief of joy; it takes our eyes off helping our children and focuses them on what you wished was happening instead of what *is* happening, which does no good! Our children have their own unique personalities, emotional and behavioral issues, and life struggles. I'll never forget my best friend asking her other friend for advice on how to handle a rebellious child, and her friend answered, "I don't know. My children have never rebelled against me before." I've always laughed at this story because all children and parents are different.

Do stay calm and step away if needed.

Your children will have struggles as they grow. There is nothing that pains us more as parents than our children hurting, but mixing our anxiety and emotion into their struggle only causes more issues. Scientists at Harvard University conducted a study called the "Still Face Experiment," which showed that children are deeply affected by the social interaction and facial expressions of their parents. This means it's okay to be upset when our children are hurt, disruptive, angry, embarrassing, or disrespectful, but remaining calm and rational in the midst of an emotional storm is a powerful tool. If you find yourself out of control and angry, step away until you calm down. There is nothing productive that comes from parenting when we are acting like a child ourselves.

Get to the root of the misbehavior.

Sure, you see screaming and kicking. You hear cussing or stomping. You hear "You're a horrible parent." But beneath those words and actions, there is more at the root. Godly parents know misbehavior is like an onion, and our job is to peel back the layers and get to the core. Ask yourself what is going on in your child's heart. Are they tired? Hungry? Stressed? Needing your attention? Feeling rejected? Whatever it is, get to the root of it. (See chapter 13, page 106, for more tips.)

Stay in the moment. Don't jump to the future.

When your toddler is throwing food at you or your teenage son is slamming the door in your face, you might jump ahead in your mind to your son heading to juvenile detention center. But don't do that. Although it is normal for parents to worry, most difficult phases are just that, phases, which means you need to deal with the behavior in front of you and not panic that your son's behavior will continue to progress.

Don't lose sight of the long-term goal of parenting.

For example, if a child is acting out on the bus due to ADHD, consider ways to help him make better decisions in the short term, knowing that your day-to-day focus on these struggles will give him the long-term skills he needs to succeed once he leaves the home. As parents, we may not always see the instant progress we desire, but we can still believe their future will reap the reward.

FOR REFLECTION

When people addressed issues with Jesus, he didn't dismiss them. Instead, he jumped into their story, asked questions about their issues, and acted on it. As parents, when our children are acting out, we want to do the same for them.

What is my long-term plan for my son's character and behavior? Is my parenting supporting this?
Think about what your long-term goals are for your son in 5 months, 5 years, 15 years and so on. Are the actions you are choosing helping support your goal?

Does my son need more grace for his behavior? Or am I giving too much?
Jesus gives us grace and mercy for our mistakes, albeit we often have to pay the consequences of sin. Sometimes our children can grow in their faith by our giving them grace when they do not deserve it, as Jesus does for us. However, if grace is met with disrespect and defiance, then other methods are necessary.

Do I need to seek outside help for my son's behavior?
Sometimes you may need to involve a therapist, pastor, or friend when you feel at a loss for handling your son's challenging behavior. Remember: It's okay to ask for help from others.

Final Thoughts

The other night, I was lying in bed with one of my sons at bedtime. We were looking at his old preschool artwork we had just found, when I looked down at his cheek and noticed a tear.

I instantly pulled him away from me to look into his eyes to see if he was okay. "What's wrong, babe? Why are you crying?"

He said, "Sometimes it feels sad to know I'm growing older." Not surprisingly, his tears made me emotional, and I just hugged him close again.

As I sat there with him, I reminded him that even though God intends for children to grow up, I will never stop being his mom—even when I'm old and gray. I thought of my mom, who I still call each day because she is so special to me, and reflected on the beautiful role of what a parent is.

People always desire purpose on this earth, and today I pray that you see the amazing purpose God has given you in raising a son. The world needs more world-changers, and we change the world each day we invest in parenting our sons with God's love.

As we close this book together, I pray its words have encouraged you and equipped you in the parenting of your son, and that you will use it when you need parenting tips and go to God when you need more. And I pray that one day your own son will lead his children to a relationship with Christ because of all you've given him in his life.

Love,
Quinn

RESOURCES

Books to Increase Parenting Knowledge

- Chapman, Gary. *The Five Love Languages*
- Doucleff, Michaeleen. *Hunt, Gather, Parent*
- Evans, Jimmy. *The Four Laws of Love*
- Gottman, John. *Raising an Emotionally Intelligent Child*
- Magruder, Jana. *Nothing Less: Engaging Kids in a Lifetime of Faith*
- Sax, Leonard. *Boys Adrift*
- Sax, Leonard. *The Collapse of Parenting*
- Tripp, Tedd. *Shepherding a Child's Heart*

Online Resources and Websites

5lovelanguages.com/quizzes/love-language
To find your child's love language

fightthenewdrug.org
For information and resources on pornography prevention

digitalfuturesinitiative.org
For programs that help children fight modern digital issues like bullying, texting, driving, and relationships

the techmum.com/2019/06/14/family-technology-contract
For downloadable technology contracts

bark.us or covenanteyes.com
For more information about phone and technology filters

REFERENCES

Centers for Disease Control and Prevention. "Anxiety and Depression in Children: Get the Facts." Accessed September 7, 2021. CDC.gov/childrensmentalhealth/features/anxiety -depression-children.html.

Centers for Disease Control and Prevention. "Developmental Milestones." Accessed September 7, 2021. CDC.gov/ncbddd /childdevelopment/positiveparenting/middle2.html.

Chapman, Gary. *The Five Love Languages*. (Illinois, Northfield Publishing, 1992), 35–119.

CPR News. "How To Get Kids To Do Chores: Does The Maya Method Work?" September 1, 2018. Cpr.org/2018/09/01/how -to-get-kids-to-do-chores-does-the-maya-method-work.

Dean, Lucy. The Hobbies that Boost IQ by 10%. February 1, 2021. au.finance.yahoo.com/news/the-hobbies-that-boost-iq-by -10-232531314.html.

Dicheva, Diana, "How to Cultivate a Secure Attachment with Your Child, *The Greater Good Magazine*, February 2, 2017. Greater-good.berkeley.edu/article/item/how_to_cultivate_a_secure _attachment_with_your_child.

Dowshen, Steven. (Reviewed by) "Understanding Puberty." Accessed September 17, 2021. kidshealth.org/en/parents /understanding-puberty.html.

Evans, Jimmy. *The Four Laws of Love*. Texas: XO Publishing, 2019. 21.

G., Deyhan. "How Much Time Does the Average American Spend on their Phone in 2021?" Updated November 21, 2021. Techjury .net/blog/how-much-time-does-the-average-american -spend-on-their-phone/#gref.

Gaultiere, Bill. "Jesus Set Boundaries." Accessed October 20, 2021. Soulshepherding.org/jesus-set-boundaries.

Goldman, J. "Ed Trotnick and the Still Face Experiment." October 18, 2010. Scienceblogs.com/thoughtfulanimal/2010/10/18/ed -tronick-and-the-still-face.

Got Questions. "What does the Bible Say About Christian Character." Accessed October 10, 2021. Gotquestions.org /Christian-character.html.

Grazer, Brian and Charles Fishman, *A Curious Mind: The Secret to a Bigger Life*. New York: Simon & Schuster, 2015. 12.

Heckler, Lorna and Wetchler, Joseph. *An Introduction to Marriage and Family Therapy*. New York: The Haworth Clinical Practical Press, 2003. 18–20.

Ingram, Chip. "Five Characteristics of Biblical Discipline." Focus on the Family. August 30, 2019. Focusonthefamily.com /parenting/five-characteristics-of-biblical-discipline.

Johnson, John. "What to Know About Toxic Masculinity." June 21, 2020. MedicalNewsToday.com/articles/toxic-masculinity.

Laule, Sara. (Reviewed by). "Masturbation and Young Children." Accessed September 18, 2021. MottChildren.org/posts/ your-child/masturbation-and-young-children.

National Bullying Prevention Center. "Bullying Statistics." Last modified November 2020. Pacer.org/bullying/info/stats.asp.

National Center for Education Statistics. "Table 5.14. Number of instructional days and hours in the school year, by state: 2018." Accessed on September 16, 2021. Nces.ed.gov /programs/statereform/tab5_14.asp.

National Institute of Mental Health. "The Teen Brain: 7 Things to Know." Accessed October 2, 2021. Nimh.nih.gov/health /publications/the-teen-brain-7-things-to-know#pub4.

Neil, Bradbury. "Attention span during lectures: 8 seconds, 10 minutes, or more?" *The Advances in Physiological Education 40*, issue 4. (December 2016): journals.physiology.org/doi/full /10.1152/advan.00109.2016.

Net Nanny. "The Detrimental Effect of Pornography on Small Children." December 19, 2017. Netnanny.com/blog/the-detrimental -effects-of-pornography-on-small-children.

Niiranen J, Kiviruusu O, Vornanen R, et al. "High-dose electronic media use in five-year-olds and its association with their psychosocial symptoms: a cohort study." researchportal .helsinki.fi/en/publications/high-dose-electronic-media-use -in-five-year-olds-and-its-associat.

Pew Research Center. "In U.S., Decline of Christianity Continues at Rapid Pace." October 17, 2019. Pewforum.org/2019/10/17/in-u -s-decline-of-christianity-continues-at-rapid-pace.

Prodromo, Peter. "Introducing: The Impulse Generation." August 6, 2019. Bostondigital.com/insights/introducing-impulse -generation.

Roux, Nicolette. "What You need to know about Young Boys' Testosterone." Accessed October 2, 2021. powerfulmothering .com/that-tricky-thing-called-testosterone.

Sax, Leonard, *Bringing Up Boys*. New York: Basic Books, 2007. 82–87.

Si, Aishwarya. Psychology Discussion. (blog) "Top 3 Factors Influencing Personality Development." Accessed September 2, 2021. Psychologydiscussion.net/personality-development -2/top-3-factors-influencing-pers\onality-development/1934.

Smietana, Bob. "Young Bible Readers More Likely to be Faithful Adults, Study Finds." October 17, 2017. Lifewayresearch.com /2017/10/17/young-bible-readers-more-likely-to-be-faithful -adults-study-finds.

Smith, James Bryan. *The Good and Beautiful God*. Illinois, InterVarsity Press, 2009. 154.

Stop Bullying. "How to Prevent Bullying." Accessed October 25, 2021. Stopbullying.gov/prevention/how-to-prevent-bullying.

Stroufe, L. Alan, "Attachment and development: A prospective, longitudinal study from birth to adulthood," Attachment and Human Development 7, issue 4 (August 2006): 349–367, https://doi.org/10.1080/14616730500365928.

Tripp, Tedd. *Shepherding a Child's Heart by Tripp*. Pennsylvania: Shepherd Press, 1995. 146–148.

Zeltser, Francyne. "A psychologist shares the 4 styles of parenting—and the type that researchers say is the most successful." Last modified July 1, 2021. Cnbc.com/2021/06/29 /child-psychologist-explains-4-types-of-parenting-and-how -to-tell-which-is-right-for-you.html.

INDEX

V

W

Acknowledgments

As a girl who loves to encourage others, I am highly encouraged by those who have believed in me and my passions when I couldn't see it for myself. Following dreams is easy when someone says they believe in you.

For this book, I am forever grateful to my parents and sister, Kristine, for always answering the phone, and for never wavering in pointing me back to God's love for me—the best gift of my life. I am thankful for my husband, Joe, my biggest fan from the day we met, who has willingly supported me with a loving side grin through each leap I take. I'm also thankful for my sweet sons, who are the inspiration for it all—I just love you and wouldn't know what to write without you by my side. And lastly, to Alesha, Holly, Esther, and my Bible study girls—thank you for always cheering.

About the Author

QUINN KELLY, MS, LMFT is a wife to her middle school sweetheart, boymom (times four), writer, speaker, podcaster, and licensed marriage and family therapist. Her blog, Sanctification and Spitup, was birthed when she first had children. She wanted to have a place to connect with other parents in an authentic yet encouraging way through the highs and lows of motherhood. From her blog, Quinn began speaking to groups of women and men, which led her to launch her own conference series called the Renew Faith Conferences in Houston, TX. Now, with her Renew You Podcast, Quinn offers a dose of Jesus + therapy in every episode. When Quinn is not writing or seeing clients, she is shuffling her boys between swim practices and walking her goldendoodle, Hazel, who has entirely too much energy.

9 781638 072089